THE
WORKING
RELATIONSHIP

THE
WORKING RELATIONSHIP

MANAGEMENT STRATEGIES FOR CONTEMPORARY COUPLES

LISA STELCK
AND
CHERYL NEWMAN

VILLARD BOOKS NEW YORK 1986

Library of Congress Cataloging in Publication Data
Stelck, Lisa.
  The working relationship.
  Bibliography: p.
  1. Marriage.   2. Communication in marriage.
3. Interpersonal relations.   I. Newman, Cheryl.
II. Title.
HQ734.S8563 1986   646.7′8   85-40722
.ISBN 0-394-72406-2

Text design and illustrations by Mary A. Wirth
Manufactured in the United States of America
9 8 7 6 5 4 3 2
First Edition

To Boegy and Charley

Acknowledgments

We extend our greatest appreciation to our friends whose interesting lives provided background material for the book. Seven couples who took the time to experiment with the Summit process deserve particular acknowledgment. The notes and exercises they generously shared with us became the basis for many examples in the book. For their candor and trust we thank Steve and Mary Barger, Peter and Becky Coffey, Lennie Copeland and Lewis Griggs, Greg Hammer and Christina Pahl, Dave and Ann Hicks, Karen and Steve Hobbs, and Mark Horton and Megan Topping.

The Stanford Graduate School of Business was an unwitting but important contributor to the making of the book. At the G.S.B. we were introduced to many of the management concepts and practices that were ultimately incorporated into the Summit process.

A special note of gratitude to Steve Hobbs for his insightful critique of the manuscript. To Susan McGrath, whose friendship made it possible for Cheryl to continue writing after the birth of Lisa Ames. And to Kathy Schmidt for her creative input on the workbook.

For their love, we thank our families: Del and Betsy Stelck, Shirley and Paul Newman, Kristin, Beth, Donna, Jayne, and Jeff.

Our husbands offered encouragement and support from the beginning. They celebrated the excitement and helped us through the difficult times with their patience, humor, and perspective. We feel profoundly grateful to have such special men as partners.

Finally, the people at Villard Books enabled two friends with an idea and a dream to wrap words around the idea and realize the dream. Jack McKeown had faith that we could write a book when we had doubts. Laura Godfrey guided us through the final stages of editing and production. Most important, Marc Jaffe gave us a chance, because he believed in the Summit concept.

CONTENTS

PART ONE

THE SUMMIT CONCEPT

CHAPTER 1

THE EVOLUTION OF THE SUMMIT

Imagine yourself stretched out before a blazing fire in a redwood cabin nestled among snow-covered evergreens. Your partner, face glowing from this afternoon's cross-country skiing, returns from the kitchen with two mugs of steaming cider. Over the course of the day you have talked about your careers, children, health, sexual happiness, finances, and domestic responsibilities with a candor and intensity that is difficult to summon in your day-to-day lives. It hasn't all been easy, but you've gotten many things off your mind, resolved some issues that had been causing friction, and made important plans together.

Tonight you are going to prepare your partner's favorite supper. After a moonlight ski you will pop the cork on a bottle of vintage champagne and toast each other and your future. Tomorrow, after completing your talks, you plan to pack a lunch and ski to the top of the ridge for a picnic before departing. You smile at the setting—and at the renewed sense of intimacy and trust in your partnership.

Does this sound like a dream? It need not be. For this was the actual experience of friends of ours who not too long ago followed our recommendation to engage in their own private Summit conference. Like many of us—contemporary couples who find themselves swept up by the conflicting demands of work, family, personal, social, and financial considerations—they were searching for a way to manage their life together. The Summit process, as described in the following chapters and the workbook section that accompanies them, is such a way.

A Summit takes place over the course of two days in a location away from home. During those forty-eight hours, partners take stock of their lives, review past performance, plan for the future, and devise strategies for achieving their objectives. Being alone and away also gives them a chance to revitalize their emotional and physical relationship. The Summit process provides couples with a problem-solving and planning framework that encourages discussion, negotiation, and consensus. It gives partners the opportunity, through a series of insight-building exercises and discussions, to explore deeply personal concerns in an organized and meaningful way. In their Summit Talks, partners focus on the various areas of their life where conflict must be resolved and choices made. We characterize these as ten broadly defined *functional areas*: work, leisure, love, home, money, family, health, travel, environment, and friends. Within the Summit framework, partners use the internal dynamic of their relationship—mutual love, respect, and commitment—to take control and begin managing their life together.

HOW THE SUMMIT EVOLVED

LISA: "The Summit evolved as a personal response by my husband, Boegy, and me to an environment in which we seemed to be losing control. In 1981, during my second year of the MBA program at Stanford University, I began interviewing for marketing positions at firms located primarily in the Midwest and East. During that same period, Boegy began contemplating a career change and opened discussions with a number of financial firms in California. In addition to our respective job searches, we each had numerous other commitments that we were attempting to juggle. Boegy's work demanded a fair amount of travel and entertaining clients. He also was busy training for a marathon. I was a full-time student actively involved in many campus activities. We were both trying to develop new friendships while maintaining the relationships we had with friends scattered about the Bay Area. Finding time to sit down to a meal together, let alone talk seriously about the direction our lives were taking, seemed impossible. As we focused our energies on these outside demands, our personal relationship began to suffer. Trivial problems took on gigantic proportions; we found ourselves becoming easily agitated about the smallest things and overly critical of each other.

"One night, Boegy and I each returned home with news of exciting job offers. The only problem was that Boegy's offer came from a firm on the West Coast and mine from a company based in the Midwest. Suddenly it struck us: Here we were, two supposedly rational and intelligent managers from excellent business schools, doing a pitiful job of managing our life together. Our relationship was deteriorating and we were moving in different directions without a clear sense of purpose. That night we decided that the survival of our partnership depended, in large part, on our willingness to take charge like the managers we were trained to be. The time had come to discuss our professional and personal objectives in a meaningful way and to make some joint decisions about our future.

"We selected a time for a meeting and proceeded to develop a list of the things we wanted to discuss. As the date approached, our initially short agenda began to grow. Because I felt that a realistic discussion of our careers would have to include planning for children, I added that topic to the agenda. Boegy wanted to explore our long-term financial aspirations as part of the discussion. We both agreed that we should talk about the pros and cons of various geographic areas as they related to our recreational, social, and cultural interests. Boegy made a note to talk about the trip to Europe we wanted to take sometime in the next two years. I figured I might as well use this occasion to bring up my pet peeves about household duties. We jotted down several agenda items relating to our respective families and how we would spend time during holiday periods. And we both wanted to talk about ways we could improve and strengthen our relationship.

"The longer our agenda grew, the more we understood how inextricably linked were the many details of our life together and how each would be affected by our career decisions. Simply listing all these matters of concern revealed how much we did *not* know about each other despite having been together for six years. I had always assumed, for instance, that we would have children but had never heard Boegy actually say, 'Yes, I want to have kids.' Developing our agenda also made us realize how much our lives had changed over the past several years. Our concerns and priorities differed significantly from those we had when we first met. Our little meeting had evolved into a full-blown 'Summit Conference,' a term Boegy aptly coined for the event. We realized it would take days, not hours, to talk about everything on our agenda, so we canceled plans for an entire weekend. When the time came, we took the phone off the hook and settled down to the most important and complex case study imaginable: our lives.

"Boegy suggested that we begin our Summit by trying to map out our lives as we would ideally like them to unfold. So we retired to separate rooms to create individual 'Timelines,' expressing how we would like to be working, living, and spending time at various stages in our lives. We emerged forty-five minutes later, anxious to see whether our Timelines were compatible. While we were able to confirm our common goals, for the first time we could articulate how our objectives diverged or clashed, as illustrated by our Timelines. This first exercise became a backdrop for the balance of our Summit discussions.

"As we tackled the items on our agenda, we spontaneously formulated other exercises to address the topics at hand. Charts, graphs, maps, scales, and hypothetical scenarios proved to be an easy and fun way to explore new ideas and share our thoughts. In discussing careers, for instance, we agreed to describe an idealized workweek. Boegy admitted that he would like to run to work with his dog, don corduroys and a sweater, and, with his dog at his feet, work at a desk looking out over the foothills surrounding Stanford. Although that kind of job opportunity did not appear imminent, the description gave us some insights about his need for a work style that permitted independence, flexibility, and individuality. Identifying the appealing characteristics of a perfect workweek eventually enabled us to focus on jobs and even specific companies that might satisfy those objectives.

"An additional benefit of the exercises was that they provided a nonthreatening medium that facilitated discussion about sensitive topics. Sex, for instance, was a subject we were somewhat hesitant to broach. We agreed to begin with a simple exercise in which we each described the most romantic evening we could imagine. It was great fun to indulge in such fantasy. More important, our written descriptions provided new insights into our respective notions of romance. Next, we each compiled a list of sexual or romantic things we wished would happen more often. This exercise gave us the opportunity to communicate areas of dissatisfaction in a gentle way, while illustrating how our individual expectations and definitions of sex and romance differed. These exercises opened the door for a frank and productive exchange about our love life.

"Our Summit talks were not without moments of frustration and anger. Strong differences of opinion surfaced in several areas. Boegy was adamant in his desire to spend weekends away from home camping, hiking, skiing, or cycling. I, on the other hand, viewed the weekend as a time to relax around the house, putter in the garden, run errands, get together with a few friends, catch up on work. I was increasingly reluctant to go away because I wanted to spend time with business school friends whom I might not see again after graduation. We also had a heated discussion about the division of household duties. I admitted how resentful I was about the time he spent training for a marathon. He told me how angry he was about the amount of time I spent at business school social activities, time that was taken away from the two of us.

"Despite the occasional low points, some yelling, and more than a few tears, it was a great relief to finally clear the air after months of misunderstanding. We made it through the weekend with our marriage and relationship not only intact, but stronger than ever. Our first Summit acted as a catalyst for decisions about our careers. I decided that my real interest lay in pursuing an idea for an entrepreneurial venture—a preschool child care center for two-career couples. Boegy decided to narrow the focus of his job search to the venture capital field. Concomitant with those career resolutions, we agreed to remain in the San Francisco Bay Area, where the opportunities for both of us seemed most ideal. We decided to postpone having children for at least several years. We devised strategies to revitalize and maintain relationships with friends and to fulfill obligations to our respective families. Travel plans were hatched for the coming year, contingent upon job developments. We negotiated a new division of labor in the house. We even developed some guidelines for spending time together.

"Although we were not exactly aware of it at the time, the 'Summit process' provided a perfect way to identify, negotiate, and resolve the concerns that were starting to threaten our relationship. The act of developing an agenda forced us to define the issues. The format of the weekend—privacy, the absence of distractions, a stretch of uninterrupted time—gave us the opportunity to focus on areas of our life that we had neglected for too long. The exercises allowed us to share information in a way that brought new insights while keeping the weekend lively. Our commitment to our marriage gave us the incentive to search for answers that would be mutually beneficial without totally sacrificing individual aspirations and needs. Certainly, some of the solutions we devised and the choices we made were compromises. But because we evaluated the alternatives and made the final decisions together, we were both committed to making them work.

"The notes we compiled throughout the weekend were translated into action plans and a calendar for the coming year, ready to be posted as reminders of the plans we made. We adjourned our Summit Meeting with a renewed sense of partnership and commitment to each other. We felt excited about our future and clear about our priorities. We knew we would continue to face difficult challenges, but felt as if we were taking control of our lives."

CHERYL: "Some months after Lisa and Boegy had completed their first Summit, Charley and I joined them for dinner. During the course of the evening the conversation turned to a topic that had invited many a lively debate in the past: How to reconcile the conflicting demands of careers, friendships, and eventual parenthood. Charley and I were in the midst of planning our wedding and a move to a new home. At the same time, we were struggling with Charley's increasing desire to change jobs and my longing to move out of the corporate world into my own business. As a result of these pressures, we were finding it more and more difficult to meet friends or spend a weekend away by ourselves. Our life seemed to be getting out of control. Neither of us had anticipated just how difficult it would be to manage our time together once we had committed ourselves to a long-term relationship.

"The conversation that evening took an unexpected turn. In response to our concerns, they enthusiastically described their recent Summit Meeting. Such a systematic approach to reviewing the state of a relationship, complete with agendas, exercises, and action plans, initially seemed alien to Charley and me. Yet as we listened to Lisa and Boegy's encouraging report, we were willing to acknowledge there might be some merit to the Summit concept. After another hour of questions about how the process worked and how we might adapt it to our concerns, we asked to borrow their agenda and the Summit Exercises they had created. We scheduled our first Summit for New Year's weekend, a month before our wedding.

"In reviewing our friends' notes, we decided that some of their agenda items were relevant to our lives, while others were not. Charley and I were at a different stage in our relationship than Lisa and Boegy. We had known each other as undergraduates at Dartmouth, lost touch for a few years, then met again when I was working as a management consultant in New York. We had a bi-coastal relationship for a year until I moved to San Francisco. After six months in the same city, we were planning to get married.

"Many topics they had not addressed were high on our list of items for discussion. While Boegy and Lisa were determined to spend at least five years in the Bay Area, Charley and I planned a more peripatetic life-style. Rather than discuss where and how to buy a house, we wanted to talk about how to make a move overseas, what geographic areas were most interesting, whose job would get us there, and when we might return to the States. As part of that discussion, we also wanted to talk about when to have a family, what our financial needs would be, and what kind of career planning we had to do to achieve our goals.

"Once our agenda was set, we perused the Summit Exercises Lisa and Boegy had loaned us. We adapted some of them to fit our interests, discarded others, and developed some exercises of our own. Charley and I decided that we could use the time at our Summit most efficiently if we completed our exercises before we began the meeting. So we each made time in our busy schedules to respond to the thought-provoking exercises.

"As the date of our Summit approached, we grew somewhat apprehensive, joking that perhaps we had better wait until after the wedding. The prospect of actually talking to each other about intense and far-reaching topics for most of two days was intimidating. Would we discover that we did not know each other as well as we thought? Could we be jeopardizing our relationship by delving into unexplored subject areas? Our curiosity about what we would discover persuaded us to forge ahead.

"Lisa and Boegy had offered us the use of their house for our Summit. We wanted to be away from our own apartment but in comfortable surroundings where we knew we would not be disturbed, so we had planned our Summit for a weekend when Lisa and Boegy would be out of town. After we arrived and settled in front of the fire, we were overcome with indecision. Should we launch into a discussion of the first exercise immediately, or wait until we felt more at ease? We hadn't imagined how difficult it would be to start. Even though I had majored in psychology in college and later studied organizational behavior at business school, I was not sure that I wanted to apply the communication 'techniques' I learned there to my own relationship. It seemed that I should not have to work so hard just to talk with Charley.

"He was the first to acknowledge that something felt a little strange. I suggested that to relieve the initial awkwardness, we should simply talk about how we were feeling at that moment. I told Charley that I was nervous about what he might reveal in the course of the next two days, afraid that it would upset me or make me angry. I knew that my tendency in either case was to withdraw, and that would impede the progress of our discussions. What if he started teasing me in the manner he knows bothers me most? Would I be able to guess what he was really trying to say? Charley expressed his concern that I might unveil a long list of complaints that I had silently harbored during the two years of our relationship. Or perhaps I would reveal a secret desire to move back to the East Coast and start a family immediately—something Charley was not prepared to do at that point in his life.

"Sharing these concerns helped us understand that certain aspects about the way we communicated made it difficult to talk openly. I would get perturbed, for instance, when, in the middle of a serious conversation, Charley would make a teasing remark. He, on the other hand, would feel frustrated when, in response to his 'What's bothering you?', I would reply 'Nothing.' To ensure that these things would not hinder our Summit Talks, we decided to establish ground rules for our discussions. Some of the ground rules were guidelines to discourage bad habits. Others reminded us of ways to communicate better.

"By talking about our feelings and creating our ground rules, we were getting our Summit off to a good start. Before we knew it, we were discussing our agenda topics, recognizing and identifying a number of other concerns throughout the process. Our Summit included moments of frustration as well as many hours of joy. It was fun and a revelation to be alone with each other, without other commitments tugging at us, sharing ideas and making important decisions about our life together.

"When our Summit finally concluded, we felt we had accomplished a lot. We developed a tentative plan for getting ourselves situated abroad within three to four years. We agreed on the compromises we would each be willing to make, both professionally and personally. We decided to start a family sometime in the coming two years. We developed some savings goals that would require material sacrifices in the short-term but allow for more financial flexibility down the road. We wrapped up our Summit by writing down the values we hoped would guide our life together.

"The Summit did not eliminate the challenges in our life, but it helped us put them into perspective and gave us a way to start managing them. It also provided a looking glass to the future by asking us to anticipate some of the important issues we might encounter. Perhaps most importantly, the Summit gave us the chance to reaffirm the basis of our relationship: great friendship, mutual trust, and love. And yes, our wedding took place on schedule, all the more meaningful because of our Summit experience."

THE SUMMIT BOOK

Our first Summits proved to be pivotal events in our lives, and were so enjoyable that we decided to make them annual events. Each year we would spend one weekend at a Summit with our partners, gauging the progress of our plans, reevaluating our priorities, analyzing new opportunities and risks, resolving conflicts, and establishing new goals. At the same time, we would rejuvenate our relationships by spending meaningful time alone as a couple. The investment in time and energy has yielded great returns.

Summits, we discovered, work best away from home—away from the pressures and reminders of other commitments. A friend's house in Berkeley, a cabin near Lake Tahoe, a lodge in Yosemite, a small inn in Vermont, a Frank Lloyd Wright house in Illinois, a lodge in Napa Valley, a hot spring resort in the mountains, and a seaside resort in Big Sur have all been memorable (and romantic) Summit sites for us. Just as the locations have varied, so has every Summit. Each one has developed its own unique character, building upon previous Summits and the interim changes in our lives. Each year our agendas seem to have a new focus, although many agenda items appear time and again. Some of the exercises have become a mandatory part of every Summit; others have been modified or replaced to reflect our changing needs. The Summit Meeting has become a high point in the year, and the Summit process an integral part of our lives.

SHARING THE SUMMIT IDEA

The idea for this book evolved over several years following our first Summits. The continuing inquiries of friends and acquaintances with whom we shared our experiences led us to realize that we were not alone in our struggle to keep our partnerships alive and well. From these friends we heard a familiar lament: "There is never enough time to do everything." We saw them trying to cope with the pressures of their careers while attempting to be loving partners and perfect parents. We watched conflicts develop as they tried to balance their role responsibilities and sort out differing expectations.

So we began to share with our friends the idea of a partners' Summit Meeting, along with our agendas and exercises. These people shared our material, in turn, with their friends. Each couple modified or interpreted our suggestions to meet their own interests and needs. Although each couple who reported back to us had experienced a unique Summit, we heard one common refrain: "We didn't realize how long it had been since we really talked."

The positive feedback we received from those who experimented with the process encouraged us to think about sharing the idea with a wider audience. As we began to put the concept into words, we realized we were drawing on some of the fundamental principles of good management that we had studied at business school. In this book, we have formalized this connection by drawing an analogy between a business enterprise and a personal partnership. The Summit concept is based on our belief that personal relationships, like businesses, can benefit from good management.

ORGANIZATION OF THE BOOK

We believed the best way to encourage couples to try the Summit process would be to keep the model simple, straightforward, and engaging. A workbook seemed to be the logical medium, hence the organization of the book. Chapters 2 through 4 discuss the challenges that contemporary couples face today, present the case for a management model adapted to those concerns, and introduce the Summit process. Chapters 5 through 8 describe each stage of the Summit process in detail, present sample exercises, and lay the groundwork for the workbook that makes up Part 3.

The Summit Workbook is designed to be used to conduct your own Summit. It includes instructions for planning your Summit, Discussion Guidelines to facilitate your Summit Talk, and ideas about how to implement your plans. In the workbook you will also find the Summit Exercises, in duplicate, for you to complete prior to your Summit Meeting.

As noted previously, to help organize the Summit Talk we have categorized the aspects of a personal partnership into ten functional areas. We do not presume to know the specific issues that an individual couple might be dealing with in their partnership, but the Summit Exercises *do* address major issues that we have found to be relevant to most couples in each of these functional areas. It is up to each couple to use the framework of the Summit to identify and address any concerns not covered by the Summit Exercises.

For those of you who are uneasy with the analogy between a personal partnership and a business enterprise, let us say that we understand. The image of a hard, rational, profit-oriented approach to a relationship frightens the romantic in us. We are not suggesting that a couple pursue this strategy in their relationship. Many successful companies today have rejected that traditional approach in favor of a looser, more people-oriented philosophy based on the belief that employee camaraderie, loyalty, and personal satisfaction are essential for corporate success. It is from this management model that couples must borrow.

For most couples today, love is simply not enough to maintain a healthy, stable relationship. A practical managerial approach is equally essential. Each couple must find the management style that works best for them. We think the Summit process has a lot to offer those who are willing to explore, experiment, and take some risks. We hope that after reading the book, you will want to try a Summit yourself. It could be one of the most rewarding investments you and your partner will ever make.

CHAPTER 2

CHANGING ROLES IN A CHANGING ENVIRONMENT

NEW ROLES, NEW OPTIONS

No one can open a news magazine or turn on the television without being confronted by the fact that couples today face ever-mounting challenges to maintaining their relationships. The risks are high: two out of five couples who exchange vows today will divorce, over half of them within seven years.[1] While the risks have increased, so have the opportunities for mutual growth within a relationship, as many of the options available to men and women today simply did not exist twenty years ago.

The risks and the opportunities couples now face result largely from the most profound social change of the past two decades: the movement of women from the home into the workplace. Social scientists, economists, and psychologists agree that the massive shift of one-half of the population has been responsible for a major upheaval in society. This transition has blurred all the well-defined roles once linked to gender, causing greater confusion and stress in contemporary relationships.

As women have moved into business, medicine, law, politics, academia, athletics, and other fields, they have accepted roles that require major commitments of time and energy. Yet most women have assumed employment responsibilities *in addition to*, not *in place of*, traditional domestic obligations. The conflicting demands of professional and domestic roles can be an ongoing source of friction between partners.

Women who choose to work at home caring for children and managing a household are not immune to conflict arising from new role options. Recognition and status for work in the home is harder to come by these days. Women we know who stay home full time report that they are considered second-class citizens. In many social groups they are effectively ignored by those who think "moms" could not possibly have anything interesting to say. One friend of ours had business cards printed with MOTHER OF THREE to underscore her belief that what she does is valuable work.

Whether she works in or out of the home, a woman today must contend with the familiar media image of the modern superwoman: Looking gorgeous and fit in her designer sweats, fresh from closing a million-dollar deal at the office, she expertly wields the sushi knife in her immaculate French Country kitchen while her impeccably kept baby plays intelligently at her feet. Does anybody fit this description? The pressure women feel to live up to this image has increased the uncertainty and tension in the lives of couples.

Male roles have also been transformed in the last decade, although not as radically. Men are assuming more domestic responsibility, participating in house-keeping and child-rearing to a greater degree than in the past. But the movement of women into the work force has not been balanced by a parallel movement of men into the home. For the most part, men have chosen to retain their traditional role as provider, working full time outside the home. That's not to say men are having an easier time weathering social change. Many men today are baffled about what they are supposed to be doing, thinking, and saying with regard to the women in their lives. Our husbands and male friends say they are confused. They are expected to be sensitive (whatever that means) as well as strong. They agree to participate in household duties, but then find themselves being criticized for folding the towels wrong. They know too many women who want independ-ence until it comes to changing tires or fixing the toilet.

CONFUSION AND CONFLICT IN THE PERSONAL PARTNERSHIP

Changing roles and new options invite internal and interpersonal conflict. In the past, traditional gender-based roles provided security by dictating not only the specific responsibilities of each partner, but also the division of power and au-thority in the relationship. When male and female roles were more distinct, prior-ities seemed clearer and the decision-making process itself was less complicated.

Most of us applaud the fact that men and women have more choices than ever before. But along with the freedom to choose comes the shared responsibility for income production, child-rearing, housekeeping, and decision-making. As a result of this dichotomy, we have trouble translating belief into action. A recent study of American couples by Philip Blumstein and Pepper Schwartz, docu-mented in their book, *American Couples*, reports that "the changing nature of male and female roles creates problems as couples go about even the most mun-dane tasks."[2] For most couples, overlapping roles and multiplying options have made dealing with even the most commonplace decisions a complex procedure with subtle psychological as well as practical implications. The impact has been felt in almost every area of the personal partnership, from managing family fi-nances to coordinating leisure time. The examples below illustrate but a few of the potential areas in a partnership where conflict can arise because of the chang-ing environment.

WORK

One question many couples face is: Should both partners work full time outside the home? Partners must weigh financial need and their individual desire for professional achievement against considerations such as the amount of time they want to devote to being together and to the smooth operation of the household. The arrival of children further complicates the picture.

A friend of ours who works in a medium-size law firm agonized about her choices after the birth of her first child. The new grandparents were confused and disappointed that their daughter was planning to return to work a month after the birth of their grandchild. But our friend's husband depended on her going back to work so that they could meet existing financial obligations as well as the costs associated with a new family member. Her female colleagues looked upon her early return as evidence that women make dependable workers and are not maternal dropouts who underutilize their advanced degrees. But her close friends from college, all of whom elected to stay home with their children, disapproved of her leaving an infant with a caretaker. She herself was uncertain about what to do. During her pregnancy, she unquestionably planned to return to the law firm following a month of maternity leave, but after the baby was born, she began to have second thoughts. Needless to say, her uncertainty was compounded by the conflicting expectations of her family, friends, and co-workers.

Today, work options are more varied than ever before. Partners who would rather not work full time can think about job-sharing, flex-time arrangements, or part-time work. Two psychologists we know each carry a partial client load and conduct several groups together so they can spend as much time as possible with their new son and each other. New technologies have made working out of the home a viable possibility for many people. We have a friend who edits books, one who designs cabinets, another who runs a children's goods catalogue business—all out of their own homes. We also know several couples who work as business partners at home. One couple produces films, another writes software programs, and another sells commodities. These examples illustrate the array of options available. But the step to a less traditional arrangement can be risky and requires a clear understanding between partners.

LISA: "Boegy and I find ourselves constantly assessing and reassessing choices for work. He prefers to work full time at a traditional job. I, on the other hand, like to work for myself, usually on a number of projects simultaneously. The problem is that none of my entrepreneurial forays have yet contributed significantly to our cash flow. So, understandably, Boegy sometimes feels as if he is working to support my adventures—and I occasionally feel guilty for not contributing more directly to the bank account. We talk regularly about my getting a salaried position. Then we remember that, in addition to the potential payoff from my endeavors, my independence and autonomy allow us to spend more time together and make me an easier person to get along with. We continue to search for the arrangement that is fair and most beneficial for us individually as well as for our relationship. The discussion is ongoing."

CHERYL: "Recent concerns that we have had about work focus on how to satisfy our long-term objectives and raise our child in an environment that includes equal participation by both parents. As a result of one pre-baby Summit discussion, we've agreed that I will work for myself, at home, while our child is young. We hope that someday Charley and I will be able to switch positions—I will pursue a career that may demand I be away from home for extended periods, while he establishes a career that allows him greater flexibility to stay at home."

For partners who are both committed to advancing their full-time careers, whose career takes priority? This toughest of issues gets particularly complicated when relocation is involved. A recent study of two-career couples by a Stanford University researcher, Dr. Wenda Brewster O'Reilly, found that if a couple moved for career reasons, it was because the husband had been offered a better job. They did not choose to relocate to advance the wife's career. Even if the move affected the woman's career negatively, these couples rationalized their decisions in economic terms: the man commands a higher salary and thus the move benefits the whole family financially.[3]

While such economic logic may be advantageous in the short term, partners must also consider the impact of their decision for the future. Will the woman's career be thwarted? What if she cannot find a job she likes? Friends of ours recently moved from Manhattan to rural Illinois because of an excellent career opportunity for the man. The woman, who was formerly in the advertising business, has not been able to find work suitable for her talents. While they both agree the decision was the right one, they admit it has put some stress on their relationship.

Deciding what kind of work to do is another important choice partners must make. Climbing the career ladder in a single company is not as common today as a generation ago when security and stability were deemed essential attributes in a job. In this day and age most people expect a lot more from work than just their paycheck. As the world explodes with new career fields, the prospects for finding personal satisfaction in a job increase. Partners must continually weigh factors such as long hours, commuting time, and heavy travel schedules against the benefits of salary, status, and potential promotion. They must reach a mutual understanding about the compromises and trade-offs they are willing to make between career and life-style to satisfy them personally while keeping the partnership intact.

MONEY

When a man was the sole source of income, he wielded all the leverage over the couple's financial circumstances. Even if a woman was delegated some responsibility for the family budget, the man usually retained final say over any decision with significant financial implications. Today things are different. Most contemporary women have worked at some point in their lives. They are accustomed to earning money and deciding how to spend it. When a woman becomes part of a couple she does not anticipate relinquishing her voice in money-related matters any more than does her partner. The *American Couples* study found that the majority of couples, no matter what their income level, argue more often about how money is to be spent than how it is to be earned or how much they have.[4]

LISA: "Boegy and I have different ideas about how to spend money. With any discretionary income, I like to buy tangible goods—sheets, clothes, furniture. Boegy prefers to purchase experiences—a massage, a hot-air-balloon ride, a soak in the Japanese baths. When it comes to selecting a gift for friends, we inevitably disagree. I want to give a copper pot; he wants to give a night at an inn."

In an attempt to avoid or resolve conflict surrounding spending and savings decisions, couples we know have devised myriad ways to handle their income. Some pool everything. Some have separate bank accounts. Others have a common account to which both contribute for shared expenses and individual accounts for personal expenditures and investments. However, these alternatives raise other questions: Do partners contribute equally to the common account or make contributions proportional to their respective incomes? Is financial decision-making shared equally regardless of the amounts contributed? What about a partner who works full time caring for children and the home? What is the value of that nonmonetary contribution and what influence does that person wield in financial decisions?

Underlying the practical issues associated with money are more subtle and complex issues about authority and trust in the relationship. Blumstein and Schwartz suggest that money symbolizes different things for men and women. For men, it confers a sense of identity and power; for women, money signifies security and autonomy.[5] For both, income appears to be correlated with influence in the partnership.[6] Because males generally earn more than their female partners, the balance of power in a relationship would appear to be tipped in favor of the male. Couples must recognize and be prepared to deal with these issues, and commit themselves to finding a workable approach to managing finances. By openly sharing concerns about money and establishing spending priorities, couples will be taking the first steps toward easing the friction that money causes in a relationship.

CHERYL: "When I began working full time on this book and taking care of our baby, I experienced some insecurity about my new role. I wondered if I was really a full partner in our relationship now that I wasn't making a financial contribution. Even though I knew I was contributing in other important ways, I felt as though Charley should make ultimate decisions about financial matters. After all, he was the only one earning the money to support us. It took a couple of emotional Summit conversations and a complete reappraisal of our roles in the relationship before I felt really comfortable participating in decisions about money on an equal basis."

FAMILY

Contemporary couples face a host of questions about children that were rarely asked a generation ago:

- Should we have children? For many couples today, professional, social, political, and other interests may take priority over raising a family. Attitudes toward childless couples have changed, and while social and familial pressure to produce offspring still exists for many couples, those who decide to remain childless are no longer considered selfish or strange.
- When should we have children? The biological time clock appears to be ticking much longer than was previously assumed. Many couples today are waiting to start a family until they are well into their thirties or early

forties. Career goals, travel plans, and emotional and financial readiness all enter into the timing decision.

CHERYL: "I had always assumed that I would have a baby before I turned thirty, and I wanted to be working for myself when that happened. Charley had not given much thought to planning a family, although he knew he wanted to do a lot more camping and winter mountaineering before becoming a father. At the time I began to feel concerned about children, we were also facing career and geographic changes. I was sure that if we tried to do everything we wanted to do before starting a family, I would be closer to forty than thirty when it happened. The result of a long and complex Summit discussion was a controlled flurry of activity, including a long-planned trip to climb Mt. Rainier, a decision about a new job for Charley, a move to a new part of the country, and the birth of our daughter five months before my thirtieth birthday."

- Who will care for our children? The demand for good child care far outstrips the supply at this point, and the cost is prohibitive for many couples. A working mother may have to consider compromising her career to provide the kind of care she wants for her child. If she does return to work full time, she may not receive the full support of family and friends. Unfortunately, working fathers have less choice. Few American companies offer paternity leave, and full-time fathering is still not considered appropriate for a man.
- What role will each of us play in raising our children? Happily, fathers are no longer restricted to the roles of disciplinarian and weekend pal. The sight of a man proudly coaching his daughter's soccer team or a mother handing a wet baby over to her husband to change is not unusual today. But with the disappearance of a strict division of labor for child care, couples must carefully articulate their individual responsibilities.

Extended family relations provide another potential source of tension for couples. Seemingly simple discussions about where to spend the holidays, for instance, can easily erupt into fights between partners. Other decisions, such as how to handle meddling relatives, or when to see children from another marriage, can lead to serious misunderstandings. Clarifying expectations and even delegating responsibility for such things as sending birthday cards can make extended family relations easier to handle and keep disagreements between partners to a minimum.

LISA: "Trying to allocate time to our respective families during the holidays caused some real tension in our relationship for a while. Boegy's parents live in Florida and mine in Southern California. For several years we attempted a mad cross-country dash on Christmas Eve in order to spend equal time with both sets of relatives. Not only were we exhausted, but neither family was wholly satisfied with the amount of time we gave them. Finally, we decided that we would alternate—spending Christmas in Los Angeles one year and West Palm Beach the next. Everyone agrees that this plan makes the holidays more relaxing and enjoyable."

ENVIRONMENT

The many alternatives available to couples today often prove to be a source of conflict when partners make decisions about life-style and environment. Deciding where to live in relation to work may involve compromise, particularly when partners hold jobs in different cities. Even when a couple lives and works in the same city, questions about the method of commuting, ownership of a car, and the type of dwelling need to be answered. When career opportunities lead partners to distant cities, the couple must decide where home is, who does the traveling, and how long the commuting relationship will last. There are many couples for whom one partner's career is dominant, but even then a major geographic change can be traumatic unless both partners are equally involved in the decision-making process. Couples today are increasingly mobile. That mobility demands that great care be taken in maintaining the life-style that is healthiest for the relationship.

LISA: "Boegy and I seem to be talking continually about where to live. Recently we discussed moving back to San Francisco from Palo Alto. I argued that if we were going to wait to have children, why not enjoy the opportunities afforded by 'city life' while we had the freedom and the money? Boegy argued that he should not have to trade his current fifteen-minute commute for an hour commute just because I wanted more action. Finally we reached an equitable compromise. We agreed to go to San Francisco at least two or three times a month and that I would take an annual trip to New York to get my dose of theater and museums."

CHERYL: "It wasn't until we had a Summit that Charley and I realized just how important our surroundings are to us. Outdoor activities, including running, hiking, and camping, are essential to our mental and physical health. Since living in different places is going to be part of our lives for a while, we established a list of priorities to which we refer whenever we explore new areas to live. So far, we have been able to find a home near an urban park and within a few hours of good camping and hiking in each new place, enabling us to resume our usual activities quickly."

LOVE

Perhaps no subject has as many dimensions as love. Creating and sustaining a good sexual and romantic relationship is a continual challenge for most couples. For busy people, the lack of time to be together is often the first obstacle. Partners who find that their paths cross erratically and only occasionally must use those brief moments alone wisely, in ways that are satisfying and meaningful to both partners.

The arrival of children changes a couple's sexual and romantic relationship. A new baby can consume the physical and emotional energy formerly directed at a partner, leading to disappointment, misunderstanding, and tension. Later on, children in the home may make parental privacy a rare luxury.

CHERYL: "Having a baby is wonderful, but it has severely limited the time that we have to nourish our relationship romantically. We decided that a new tradition in our family will be for us to celebrate our wedding anniversary away from home, family, and friends. Maybe in about fifteen years we'll be willing to share this occasion with others, but for now it is a much-needed escape from the demands and constraints of parenthood, as well as a perfect occasion for our annual Summit. It presents an opportunity to renew our marriage vows and enjoy one another's company without all the interruptions that are a necessary aspect of raising children."

Changing attitudes about sexual roles can also create problems. In the bedroom, as in other areas of life, traditional notions about male dominance and female passivity have been discarded. Yet many women and men continue to experience some ambivalence and insecurity about appropriate roles and behavior as they seek to develop a mutually satisfying sex life.

Because of the emotionally charged and sensitive nature of the topic, couples need to take time outside the bedroom to talk about their love life. Otherwise, sex becomes a weapon, and the bedroom a battleground for power and control in the relationship. Assumptions about sexual preferences, frequency, romance, foreplay, etcetera, need to be examined openly to highlight the different perceptions of each partner. Partners must clarify and define terms in order to accurately express their own needs. As difficult as it might be, talking about these issues helps build the trust and mutual understanding that is the foundation for a good physical and emotional relationship.

LISA: "For a while it seemed as if I was the one calling the shots in our sexual relationship, arranging it around *my* schedule. I was uncomfortable wielding that sort of one-sided power and worried that I was not satisfying Boegy's needs. Boegy was not totally happy with the situation but did not want to pressure me. As a result of our Summit discussions, we pinpointed the problem as a preoccupation with work that crowded out feelings, particularly during the week. We agreed to strive to be more relaxed, flexible, and democratic about initiating sex and set aside time on the weekends to be close."

HOME

Housework provides another potentially divisive issue for couples. Women who work full time outside the home can no longer accept sole responsibility for maintaining and running a home. While males agree in principle, in reality, women still bear the major responsibility for the care of the house. Even among two-career couples who profess egalitarian social ideals, including dividing the housework equally, shared responsibility remains a myth.[7] Women who do *not* work outside the home spend an average of eight hours per day on housework and children, while women who do work outside the home spend just under five hours a day. Regardless of whether their wives work, men have never been found to spend more than one and a half hours a day on housework and children. Women continue to perform 70 percent of all work in the home.[8]

Even when partners split responsibility for domestic tasks, different perceptions about what constitutes an acceptable level of cleanliness or completion may lead to conflict. The decision to share household tasks is no guarantee of household harmony; standards must be mutually agreed upon and carefully outlined. In their study, Blumstein and Schwartz turned up one particularly dismal finding: The more housework a married man does, the greater the conflict in the relationship.[9] They point out that this pattern might be a major barrier to the reorganization of roles in the home. Each couple has to devise a personal solution for maintaining their home that will satisfy their cleanliness quotient, budget, schedule, and sense of fairness. Defining standards and determining how best to meet them takes discussion and perhaps some hard bargaining.

LISA: "For several years we went through tedious arguments about household responsibilities. Both of us hated cleaning and hated fighting about it. Then we hired a housekeeper. Despite the added expense, it was one of the best decisions we ever made for the health of our relationship."

CHERYL: "Charley and I have agreed that one of our main goals in life is to simplify, especially our domestic life. The strategies we have devised to reach that goal are many. For example: all bills are paid on the same day, once a month; we clean our home thoroughly whenever important guests are expected, but suffice with expending minimal effort in the interim; our furniture is versatile and easy to care for; we don't wear shoes at home, both because it's more fun and the floors don't get as dirty!"

LEISURE

Time is a valuable commodity for partners today, particularly when both work outside the home. Careers that demand evening and weekend hours or extensive travel can make it tough for partners to enjoy outside interests. When partners do find extra time in the evening or on weekends, often it must be spent running errands, catching up on the mail, or paying the bills.

CHERYL: "During the week I am home full time, working and taking care of our daughter. Charley's business requires him to travel. Thus, Monday through Friday we keep in touch by telephone. (We learned to survive by telephone during nearly a year of managing a commuting marriage between Chicago and San Francisco.) When Charley gets home there are countless domestic details that demand our attention—for example, financial decisions, correspondence with family and friends, planning the next week's round of business trips. After allowing for the time we spend with our daughter, there literally are minutes left when we can be alone together. We feel lucky just to have a conversation. Our 'leisure' hours are usually planned by the quarter hour, and even then we rarely get to do everything we want."

Trying to decide how much free time to spend together can lead to controversy, especially because women appear to enjoy being alone more than do their male partners. This has been confirmed in many conversations with female friends who say they would like a little more time just to be by themselves.

How do couples decide how much time to devote to the pursuit of individual interests without neglecting the need for togetherness? The answer to this question is usually compromise. We have a friend who took up golf, a sport he detests, simply because it allowed him to spend time with his wife, who is an avid golfer. She, in turn, agreed to accompany him to the season's basketball games.

LISA: "Boegy likes the mountains, I like the beach. I love the theater, Boegy falls asleep. Boegy enjoys backpacking, I prefer museum hopping. I could dance until three in the morning, Boegy tries to be in bed by eleven so he can get up early and run. I like to throw big parties, Boegy prefers intimate dinners. I love dressing up in formal clothes. Boegy likes jeans, a flannel shirt, and tennis shoes. It's not always easy deciding how to spend our free time if we want to be together."

Vacations can be another subject requiring negotiation. With limited time and money, how should partners decide where to spend vacations? Friends of ours devised a workable solution to an ongoing debate about where to go. Each plans one trip a year. Inevitably, they end up spending one week sailing and one week in an exotic city. Many people like to spend some vacation time without their partner. To minimize jealousy or resentment, these decisions require a clear understanding and mutual agreement between partners.

While we all want spontaneity in our lives, many leisure-time activities do require planning. Someone has to make the reservations, buy the tickets, send out the invitations, plan the meal, or whatever is necessary to make the experience happen. Thinking ahead, establishing priorities, and delegating responsibility is necessary if busy couples want to spend their leisure time in ways that are valuable to them. Decisions about how to spend leisure time are strictly personal, but reaching them may require serious discussion.

TAKING CHARGE

Changing roles, a shifting power struggle within the relationship, new values, and conflicting expectations make maintaining a relationship seem overwhelming at times. In order to thrive, perhaps merely to survive, couples must find an effective way to make meaningful choices and plan for their future.

Assistance for couples who are trying to cope with the challenges of a contemporary partnership is increasingly available. Personal growth seminars and weekend encounters are offered under the auspices of churches and synagogues, human potential institutions, and private consultants. Psychologists, psychiatrists, and counselors who specialize in marriage and family issues offer professional help. Educational institutions sponsor panel discussions about dual-career issues during which couples share personal experiences and practical solutions.

Businesses are beginning to recognize the impact of family well-being on job performance and are offering counseling and seminars on the topic to their employees. Bookstores are full of books that offer advice about interpersonal issues.

Yet all of these resources cannot absolve the couple of the responsibility of making choices that fulfill each partner's objectives while sustaining a healthy, loving relationship that satisfies mutual goals. Is there hope for couples striving to maintain and develop a partnership in this complex world? We think so. Success is within reach of intelligent, loving, committed partners. But they must begin *managing* their life together.

CHAPTER 3

A MANAGEMENT MODEL FOR COUPLES

"Manage my relationship . . . are you kidding? I manage all day at work. My marriage is different; it just happens. And that's the way I like it." That was the response of an attorney friend when we suggested that couples ought to begin managing their partnerships. His is not an uncommon reaction to the idea. Why is it that the very people who understand the lessons from America's best-run companies, embrace the techniques of high-output management, and are enraptured by Theory Z resist applying even the most basic lessons from management to their personal lives? Probably because the idea of managing a relationship contradicts every romantic tenet. The vision of two people bound solely by mutual love and caring is shattered when we think about applying to this personal realm concepts borrowed from the corporate world. Yet the fact is, love and caring may no longer be enough to sustain a relationship in an environment characterized by pressing time demands, new roles, and a multitude of options. In this era of change, a successful partnership depends upon effective management for its very survival.

LESSONS FROM BUSINESS

The business sector provides the logical place to learn about good management. In no other sphere of human activity is the pace of change more rapid and the imperative to adapt more pressing. Companies that do not anticipate and manage change find their profits deteriorating because of product obsolescence, stiffer competition, or decreased productivity. Witness the American automobile industry, whose failure to recognize the signs of consumer disenchantment with gas-guzzling cars nearly caused its own demise. Events such as the 1972 oil embargo shattered assumptions about the U.S. hold on world markets. Japan has, in a matter of a few years, captured the international lead in a number of industries that have traditionally been dominated by American companies. In addition, upstart new ventures, whose presidents wear jeans to work, have turned some corporate giants on their ears.

These rapid technological and economic changes have forced businesses to seek innovative ways of managing. In the past few years, researchers from various disciplines of management—organizational behavior, marketing, production, economics, business policy—have probed into companies here and abroad for clues to successfully managing in a changing environment. The experts have studied corporate culture, creativity, organizational design, and entrepreneurship. American and Japanese companies alike have been dissected and analyzed. The findings have been distilled into academic, as well as popular, treatises that have become managerial manifestos for companies of all sizes. Throughout the business sector, everyone, from corporate presidents to office managers, is practicing "one-minute" or "high-output" management techniques, those terms themselves suggesting the urgent need to manage effectively. One lawyer we know reports that his firm is experimenting with Japanese "quality circles" as a way to involve all employees in improving performance. Another friend, who is a dental assistant, told us that *The One-Minute Manager* was required reading in her office.

THE PERSONAL PARTNERSHIP AS AN ENTERPRISE

So what, you may be thinking. A marriage or intimate relationship is not a Fortune 500 company or a law practice. What relevance do the theories and techniques of management have for a personal partnership? Consider the similarities.

Both a personal partnership and a business enterprise require a large initial investment. For couples, that investment includes time and emotional energy in addition to the economic contribution each makes. Both personal and business enterprises involve a high degree of risk—divorce statistics rival those for business failures. Yet the opportunity for substantial returns accompanies the investment in both cases. Successful business and personal enterprises may profit not only in economic terms, but in growth, security, and satisfaction.

The contemporary partnership and the modern business enterprise operate in a dynamic and unpredictable environment that demands creative solutions to new challenges. Experimentation and untraditional approaches are viewed with increasing tolerance in both the workplace and the interpersonal realm. At one software company in Silicon Valley, the chief computer programmer works from 10:00 P.M. to 6:00 A.M., alone, and in the nude! Nobody seems overly concerned about his unique style as long as he gets his job done. Unorthodox approaches to partnership are also increasingly accepted in the personal sector. Living on opposite coasts or vacationing alone, for instance, are acceptable options for partners today if those choices contribute to the health of their relationship.

A personal partnership roughly resembles a modern business enterprise in its form and function. In a company, executives commonly preside over an organization divided into functional areas such as marketing, finance, accounting, production, and human resources. A primary managerial task involves allocating resources to the various functional areas so as to achieve the company's desired objectives. Partners are the executives of their partnership, presiding over a life that can be divided into various functional areas: work, leisure, love, home, money, family, health, travel, environment, and friends. As executives, they are required to allocate resources wisely to achieve their goals.

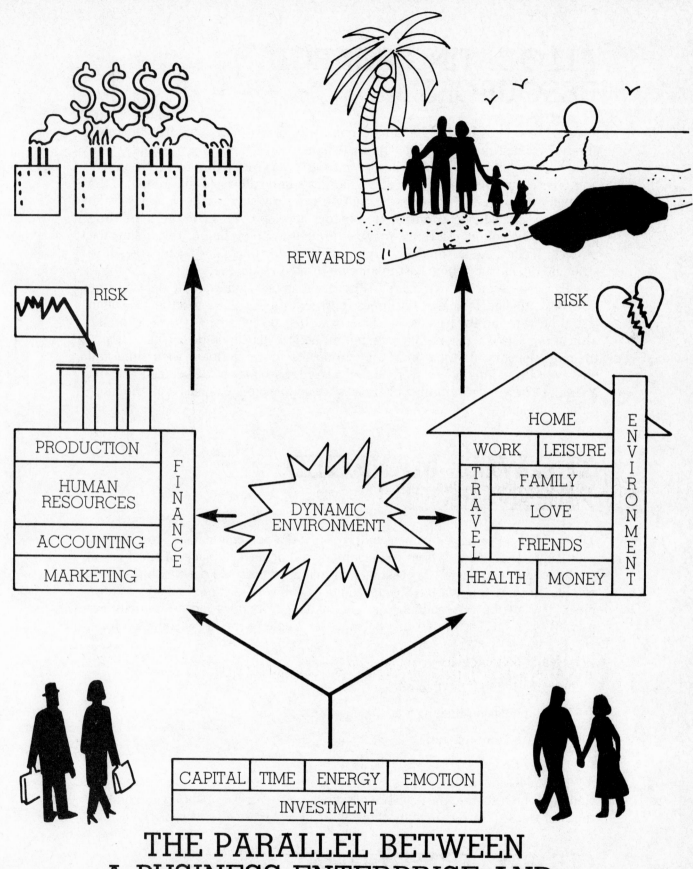

THE PARALLEL BETWEEN A BUSINESS ENTERPRISE AND PERSONAL PARTNERSHIP

ALLOCATING SCARCE RESOURCES

Because resources tend to be limited relative to needs, managers in a business enterprise must make choices. The management of a consumer products company may be forced to decide whether to fund a new marketing research project or increase the advertising budget. Resources will be allocated differently as the company matures and priorities change. In the early stages of a company's life, funds may be dedicated primarily to product development. Later, an increasing portion of the company's funds may be devoted to upgrading or expanding the physical facility. As technologies advance and markets expand, companies face strategic dilemmas in how best to allocate limited resources.

Partners resemble managers in their role as decision makers, determining how best to allocate scarce resources. Partners must decide whether to spend free time with family, friends, or alone; whether to buy a new couch or to take a vacation. The stage of the partnership influences allocation decisions. Early in their relationship, partners may want to devote the majority of their time and energy to advancing their careers. Later, a large share may be dedicated to raising a family. The growing number of choices for couples today makes it all the more difficult to allocate resources wisely.

THE WELL-MANAGED PARTNERSHIP

The parallels between a business enterprise and a personal partnership suggest that some basic lessons from management might have a place in the lives of contemporary couples. A successful, well-managed personal partnership will resemble, in some important respects, a successful, well-managed business enterprise. The attributes essential to a well-managed organization are equally important for a successful personal partnership. Some of the key attributes are:

clearly defined goals

clearly defined, flexible roles

shared decision-making

effective communication

quality time.

Couples who integrate these characteristics into their relationship will be taking the first steps toward managing their life together more effectively.

CLEARLY DEFINED GOALS

Establishing goals is the first step for couples who want to take control of their life together. Obviously, partners need to know *where* they are going before they decide how they are going to get there. Focusing on a specific goal simplifies the

BUSINESS

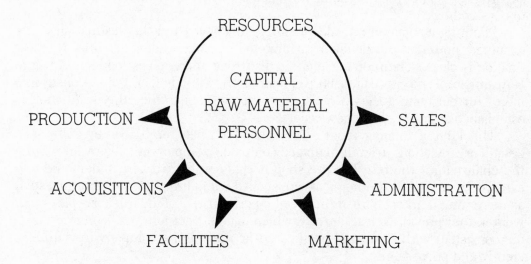

PRODUCTION

RESOURCES

CAPITAL
RAW MATERIAL
PERSONNEL

SALES

ACQUISITIONS

ADMINISTRATION

FACILITIES

MARKETING

PERSONAL PARTNERSHIP

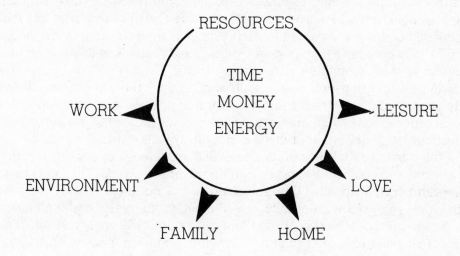

WORK

RESOURCES

TIME
MONEY
ENERGY

LEISURE

ENVIRONMENT

LOVE

FAMILY

HOME

ALLOCATING SCARCE RESOURCES

decision-making process. Because options have been limited, choices become more obvious and action more purposeful. The process of articulating goals forces partners to share their dreams and hopes, which in turn leads to greater understanding.

Planning a vacation provides a simple analogy. Until the destination is determined, no action can be taken, arrangements cannot be made. Once the destination is clear, certain options can be discarded and choices reduced. A trip to Hawaii, for instance, precludes travel by train or bike. Time or money constraints might further restrict the choice to airplane over ship. Once the destination is established, planning becomes easier.

This kind of "management by objective" has been embraced by many successful organizations. In well-managed companies, employees at every level, from the chairman of the board to the shop-floor assembly worker, understand and can articulate goals. Whether goals are spelled out in broad corporate terms, such as increasing market share, or in specific performance standards for a particular worker, they provide a clear target at which to aim. Decisions made on every level are consistent with attaining specified goals, moving the company forward efficiently and purposefully.

In business, goal setting is part of a formal planning process. Planning is usually done for an annual fiscal cycle as well as for the future. Partners can engage in a similar planning process. Short-term plans can help couples define priorities for the upcoming twelve months. Long-term plans help establish the direction of the partnership for five, ten, or twenty years into the future.

As part of the goal-setting process, couples must examine the external and internal environments to make sure their goals are reasonably attainable. Internal environmental factors are things that, to a great extent, can be controlled by the partners—for example, discretionary income or available free time. These factors might affect a couple's ability to take a trip, paint the house, or take ballroom dancing lessons. External environmental factors are variables that partners cannot necessarily control. They include such things as interest rates or the health of a family member. Those factors might influence a couple's ability to purchase a new home or move to another part of the country.

It is improbable that two people will want exactly the same thing. When goals are incompatible, partners must be willing to discuss, negotiate, and compromise in order to develop plans for the year and set the course for the future. While reaching agreement about goals is not always easy, it is essential for the health of the relationship. Without the focus that goals provide, couples can drift from opportunity to opportunity, never fulfilling their dreams. Or they may make decisions randomly, with little thought given to the ramifications for the partnership. When goals are not mutually agreed upon, partners risk making choices that are at odds with each other, threatening the stability of their relationship.

A chart showing examples of short-term and long-term goals upon which a couple might agree appears on page 27. Once goals such as these have been established, partners can begin to take action and allocate the resources necessary to achieve them. Avoiding the office on weekends, for instance, may require working late several nights or getting an extra early start in the morning. Paying off the car loan may mean fewer nights out for dinner. Running the New York marathon would require a September vacation in a spot where training can continue. Choices are easier to make because priorities have been established. Conflict is minimized because partners understand *why* they are making those choices.

GOALS IN A PERSONAL PARTNERSHIP

FUNCTIONAL AREA	GOALS	
	Short-Term	Long-Term
Work	Never at office on weekend	Business together by year 2000
Leisure	Ballroom dancing lessons	One major volunteer activity per year
Love	Dinner out together weekly	Go away together alone twice a year
Home	Hire housekeeper one day a week	Live-in help
Money	Pay off car loan	College trust for kids
Family	Spend Thanksgiving with Sue's parents	Two children within six years
Health	Run New York marathon	Maintain ideal weight
Travel	Ski vacation in spring and fall trip to Vermont	Go abroad at least every three to four years
Environment	Buy house	Move back to Seattle within ten years
Friends	See Paula and Todd once a month	Vacation with Hickses every two years

Just as strategically aware executives continually monitor the environment and modify their plans accordingly, partners must also regularly review their plans and adjust for environmental changes. Internal environmental factors, such as a decision by one partner to change careers or the arrival of a new child, will affect many areas of the partnership. External environmental factors, such as inflation or attractive new career fields, will also require partners to reassess their goals and integrate new information into their plans. By trying to envision the future, couples can shape their place in it.

You may be disconcerted by the thought of engaging in a formal planning process. Yet you certainly do some sort of planning, however sporadic and informal, in your lives now. We are simply suggesting that you formalize the process to a greater degree. Establishing goals and devising strategies to attain them does not set you on a track from which you can never deviate. Most goals will be modified numerous times as interests and outlooks change or as unexpected events occur. A dynamic environment makes that inevitable. But clearly defined, mutually agreed upon goals provide a framework for decision-making that makes it easier to avoid misunderstanding. Having a sense of the future, whether it's two months or ten years away, builds cohesiveness in a relationship and gives order and purpose to the choices partners make and the action they take. Articulating goals is the first step toward managing a personal partnership.

CLEARLY DEFINED, FLEXIBLE ROLES

Clearly defined roles is the second attribute of a well-managed partnership. In any organization, various functions and responsibilities are divided among people. Successful companies make sure each employee understands his or her role and the responsibilities that accompany that role. The chief financial officer understands that she is responsible for the fiscal health of the organization and thus cultivates good relations with investors and banks, understands the economic environment, and oversees the budgetary process with vigor. The salesperson understands that he is responsible for selling as much product as he can, representing the company to the buying public, and reporting news about competitive products and consumer demands from the field. Ideally, when each person fulfills the duties of his or her respective role, the organization functions smoothly and moves forward toward achieving its objectives.

The same is true for a personal partnership. Responsibilities must be divided between partners in order to ensure the smooth operation of the partnership. The role possibilities in a partnership are varied and numerous. They include: housekeeper, cook, child care giver, pet care giver, nurse, lover, friend, income provider, teacher, social secretary, general secretary, treasurer, host, decorator, handyperson, chauffeur, appointments secretary, community volunteer, event planner, travel agent, disciplinarian, grocery shopper, laundryperson, gardener, mechanic, electrician, plumber. Until ten or fifteen years ago it was easy to divide those roles into female and male functions. However, this is no longer the case. "Appropriate" male and female responsibilities, behaviors, and attitudes are not rigidly defined today. One result is a certain amount of chaos in the home as partners try to figure out who should do what to keep the domestic machine from breaking down. Couples must decide for themselves what roles each partner will play based on preference, aptitude, or even the flip of a coin. Sharing or alternating responsibilities is one possibility. Hiring outside help is another. Partners must understand and carry out their respective domestic roles if the partnership is to function smoothly.

Roles define what people do, but also influence how they feel about themselves. Well-managed companies seem to instill in every employee, from the telephone operator to the shipping clerk, a sense of worth and pride in the job they do. As couples work out the division of responsibility for the practical maintenance of the partnership, they must recognize the way each role contributes to the vitality of their life together. This may require an examination of the more subtle roles that keep the relationship healthy. In addition to identifying roles, partners need to claim and give credit to themselves and each other for fulfilling them.

Life and loving relationships are not static, so the roles partners assume must be inherently flexible. Couples must be able to modify, adapt, swap, add, and eliminate various roles in their partnership when the status quo is disrupted. Change is inevitable, but unexpected change can quickly destabilize a relationship, whether the changes are positive or negative.[10] An unexpected increase or decrease in salary, for example, can be equally damaging to a relationship. Paradoxical as it sounds, partners must build a high degree of flexibility into their roles.

Defining roles is not easy. Guilt, anger, resentment, confusion, and insecurity are bound to be part of the sorting-out process. Partners who are willing to experiment and explore, however, will eventually discover the roles that each must assume to support their individual needs and the goals of the partnership.

SHARED DECISION-MAKING

Today's successful organization is more likely to resemble a network of loosely connected structures than the traditional corporate pyramid. As organizations have become more horizontal in form, control and decision-making have become less hierarchical. The old "top down" chain of command has been modified by a process of consensual decision-making that takes into account the views of those who will be responsible for implementing policy. One positive impact of this approach is the generation of a greater number of creative proposals for problem-solving. Because they know the line better than anyone, assembly workers can suggest valuable ideas for improved productivity. Salesclerks can offer important insights into how better to meet consumer needs because they have daily contact with the customer.

More important, employee involvement helps ensure the successful implementation of a decision. Those who have shared in the decision-making process are more likely to accept and support the final decision, whatever it may be. Japanese industrial success has been built, in large part, upon the recognition that participation leads to productivity. Thomas Peters and Robert Waterman discovered, in their search for corporate excellence, that, indeed, productivity through people is a guiding principle in America's best-run companies.[11] Most well-managed companies are people-oriented—all ideas are carefully considered and each employee is viewed as a partner in the enterprise. This theory of participatory management suggests that if the individual succeeds, the organization succeeds.

Shared decision-making is also an essential principle for couples. When both partners lead active, valuable lives with economic and emotional consequences for the partnership, both must have a choice in the decisions that affect the partnership. In the past, a woman's life was viewed as secondary to her husband's career. She was expected to acquiesce to the demands of his professional life even if it meant continually uprooting the family or sacrificing her personal aspirations. Similarly, a man was barred from much of the decision-making in the domestic realm, regardless of his interest. Overlapping roles make that kind of unilateral approach unacceptable to most partners today. Men want a say in how the children are raised, just as women want a voice in financial planning. Partners share the risks, responsibilities, and rewards of their relationship; it makes sense that they share the decisions that affect both their lives.

As in the corporate world, a consensual approach means more creativity in problem-solving and planning. Two partners will bring two different perspectives to bear on each issue that must be resolved. Knowing that their personal view has been considered is likely to make each partner more willing to compromise and develop a mutually acceptable agreement. Both partners will then support the implementation of the final decision.

In attempting to reach consensus, a couple must often weigh each partner's individual desires against the needs of the relationship itself. At times, individual sacrifice might be required for the good of the partnership. Friends of ours who found they simply could not juggle careers, a baby, a home, their relationship, and two large animals finally decided to give away their beloved dogs. It was a painful decision for them, but they knew something had to give if their relationship was to survive the stress. In another couple, one partner decided not to accept a job promotion because it involved adding more travel to an already hectic work schedule—a move that the couple felt might snap an already fragile relationship. Finding just the right balance to satisfy individual needs and the joint mission of the partnership takes work. But when partners solve problems and make decisions together, they can develop solutions they both feel are workable and just.

EFFECTIVE COMMUNICATION

The single most important element of good management is effective communication. Without it the other managerial activities cannot take place. Communication in the business world takes a variety of forms. A board meeting governed by a strict agenda constitutes a formal and structured way of communicating. A spontaneous brainstorming session over the coffeepot is informal. Both can be effective ways of exchanging information. And both are necessary aids to decision-making and planning.

In a personal partnership, good communication is essential for planning, defining roles, and making wise decisions. However, couples today appear not to be talking, much less communicating. One recent study revealed that partners who both work outside the home spend an average of only fifteen minutes a day talking to one another.[12] Fifteen minutes—even an hour—per day is not sufficient time for partners to exchange all the information (feelings, thoughts, opinions, facts) that keep two people attuned to one another. The result, in many partnerships, is a communication breakdown.

When partners don't talk to each other small annoyances can balloon into seemingly major issues. If feelings are not expressed, anger and resentment develop. Frustration is channeled into unproductive forms of communication such as leaving a pile of dirty clothes in the middle of the room or intentionally coming home late. Those primitive forms of communication are likely to elicit responses that do little to resolve the underlying problems. Tension may finally erupt into a fight or fester beneath the surface, causing partners to withdraw from each other. The more partners lose touch, the more difficult it becomes to reopen the lines of communication. In the meantime the relationship suffers.

In a well-managed partnership, effective communication depends on sharing thoughts and feelings honestly in a neutral format. It involves developing and discussing options. It requires negotiating mutually agreeable decisions and creating workable plans. In the course of busy lives, partners cannot accomplish this kind of communication unless they schedule regular talks dedicated to these tasks. Getting away from such distractions as the telephone helps immensely. So does keeping a list of the things that need attention. Even then, communication takes a lot of effort and practice.

Most people we know think they should not have to formalize communication to this extent. We disagree. We are not suggesting that structured discussions should take the place of the informal exchanges you have over the dinner table or in bed. Rather, they should provide a complementary form of communication, a means of ensuring that all the issues affecting the partnership get the attention they deserve. Partners who communicate effectively are more likely to be in agreement about their goals, content with their roles, and satisfied with the choices they have made for their partnership.

QUALITY TIME

Many well-managed, innovative companies provide opportunities for co-workers to play together in a relaxed and enjoyable environment. Around Silicon Valley, for example, one can find everything from on-site volleyball courts to picnic grounds for the employees. At one well-known firm, employees must drop whatever they are doing at 4:00 on Friday afternoon to attend the weekly beer bust. These are more than corporate perks. They are experiences designed to build team spirit and a sense of belonging among people who would otherwise rarely talk to one another. These opportunities are provided because management understands that high-quality, nonwork time is essential to employee satisfaction, which translates into productivity on the job.

This attribute has great relevance for the personal partnership. One of the hardest things for busy partners to do is to find enough time for the two of them—away from the demands of family and work—to play, relax, have fun, and enjoy each other. The amount of quality partners' time necessary to keep a relationship vital is purely subjective, as is the way that time is used. It may be a time for making love, taking an early morning bike ride, or simply sharing a bottle of wine. It should be a time for partners to "connect" in whatever way works for them.

With so many demands vying for attention, couples may have to actually schedule time to be together. There's nothing wrong with reserving a time to meet in bed. Occasional weekends away can work wonders for a relationship. By nurturing intimacy and romance, partners strengthen the bonds that connect them. The feeling of friendship and sense of contentment that come from knowing you are loved make it easier to face the challenges of a dynamic world. An essential part of managing is making sure that high-quality time is an integral part of the relationship.

THE SUMMIT AS A MANAGERIAL TOOL

The goal of managing a personal partnership is to create a relationship in which the needs of each individual are met while the partnership flourishes. A well-managed partnership is vital and healthy, with a sense of order and control in the present and a vision for the future. It is characterized by camaraderie, mutual respect, fairness, excitement, and integrity.

Although a personal partnership is influenced by a variety of external economic, sociological, and other factors, it is mainly affected by the decisions we make. Managing requires making choices; coordinating, controlling, and allocating resources. Good management entails establishing goals, defining roles, sharing the decision-making, communicating effectively, and spending quality time together. How can partners begin to integrate these concepts into their life? The Summit process provides one way.

THE SUMMIT SOLUTION

We believe that most couples have the desire and capacity to manage their life together. We think they can take control, work out disagreements, and make wise choices. But in order to do so partners need a way to communicate, explore, and resolve at an early stage and on a continuing basis, the conflict and tensions that arise from new roles. They need a way to help them make decisions and plan rationally, taking into account the needs of each individual and the needs of the partnership. They need a problem-solving and planning framework that is flexible enough to be adapted to their unique relationship and work within the time constraints of their active lives. The Summit process provides that structure.

The Summit is not based on any one dogma, specific theory, or precise technique, nor does it require special training. It integrates proven managerial methods with common sense and practical experience. It asks partners to assume responsibility for the success of their relationship by using the knowledge each has of him or herself and partner to devise solutions that will help realize the potential of the partnership. The Summit helps a couple focus on important questions, but it does not provide the answers—those must come from within. The Summit should be held in the time, place, and manner that feels most comfortable; the framework modified to suit each particular partnership. The Summit should be uniquely yours.

The Summit process is a challenging personal endeavor that requires a serious commitment. Success depends, in large part, on your willingness to summon and utilize the inner resources you possess as individuals and as a couple and to dedicate time and energy to the process. If you are willing to make that commitment, the Summit can be a powerful tool.

IS THE SUMMIT FOR YOU?

If you are intrigued by the idea of the Summit, you are probably wondering if the experience would be meaningful for your partnership. Take a moment to answer the following questions. Have your partner do the same.

1. Do you feel you spend enough high-quality time with your partner?

2. Are you satisfied with the way decisions are made in your partnership?
3. Are you satisfied with the way resources (time, money, energy) are allocated?
4. Do you have a clear set of personal goals? A clear set of objectives for your partnership?
5. Are you satisfied with the roles you and your partner play in the partnership? Do you feel you get enough credit for the things you do?
6. Are your personal needs (social, professional, recreational, physical, emotional) being met?
7. Is your relationship as balanced, comfortable, and loving as you believe it could be?
8. Are you satisfied with the way you and your partner communicate?
9. Do you feel in control of your life and the direction of your partnership?

If you both answered yes to all of the above questions, put this book away. If you answered no to even a single question, you should consider the Summit an opportunity to improve your partnership. But before you begin, you will want to understand exactly what is involved.

THE STAGES OF THE SUMMIT PROCESS

The Summit process comprises four stages that require an investment of approximately sixty hours of each partner's time.

THE SUMMIT PROCESS

STAGE ONE: THE PLANNING MEETING (1–2 HOURS)
In the first stage of the Summit process partners hold a short planning meeting. At this meeting they sign their Summit Contract, a document that signifies their mutual commitment to the Summit; decide when and where to hold their Summit Meeting; identify the areas of concern in the partnership; and develop the agenda for their Summit discussions.

STAGE TWO: THE SUMMIT EXERCISES (5–8 HOURS)
Before departing for their Summit, each partner independently completes the Summit Exercises that will provide the basis for much of their discussion. There are eighteen exercises in all, covering issues in each of the ten functional areas of a partnership. The exercises help partners organize their thoughts and ideas about these topics.

STAGE THREE: THE SUMMIT MEETING (48 HOURS)
This is the Summit: a two-day retreat dedicated primarily to talking—to resolve conflict, set goals, reach decisions, and make plans. With the help of Discussion Guidelines, partners discuss their Summit Exercises and personal agenda

topics. They translate their ideas, strategies, and commitments into Action Plans. Time is allotted for recreation and relaxation so that partners can renew their emotional and physical connection—an important part of the Summit. Although some couples find their Summit Meeting takes less time, scheduling 48 hours ensures that ample time is available for completing all the Summit activities.

STAGE FOUR: MANAGING YOUR LIFE TOGETHER (ONGOING)

The final stage of the process begins after partners return home from their Summit, when they begin to implement the decisions and plans they made. A brief Follow-Up Meeting (1 to 2 hours) several weeks after the Summit gives partners a chance to review their progress and, if necessary, revise plans or the strategies for implementing them.

THE REQUIREMENTS

Couples who are considering a Summit should be engaged in what they believe is a healthy and enduring relationship to which they are mutually committed. They must be prepared to make a substantial investment of personal resources, particularly time. It is also extremely important that both partners approach the process optimistically and energetically.

TIME

Sixty hours is a tremendous investment of time for most couples and may not be easy to find, even for something as important as your partnership. One fundamental purpose of the Summit is to provide ample opportunity to explore, in depth, issues that are too often neglected on a daily basis. Partners will be denying themselves the full benefit of the Summit if they cut corners and fail to fully complete each stage of the process.

A HEALTHY RELATIONSHIP

Another important requirement for a successful Summit is that two people feel their relationship is basically healthy. The foundation of a healthy relationship is, of course, the mutual love and caring that makes partners want to grow together, satisfy each other, and continually improve their life. A healthy relationship is built, also, on mutual trust and respect, which allow partners to express themselves openly, both intellectually and emotionally. At the Summit, partners must be able to share dreams, thoughts, desires, fears, concerns, and weaknesses without hesitation. Trust gives two people the security to explore new ideas, challenge each other, and experiment with change. Mutual respect gives partners the ability to listen for understanding, accept differing opinions and perspectives, and allow each other equal opportunity for sharing thoughts.

Partners who believe they have a healthy relationship should feel secure about their ability to handle the demands of the Summit process. Couples who question the fundamental health of their partnership should postpone their Summit. If two people are contemplating separation or feeling extremely vulnerable, they are unlikely to find the Summit a productive experience. In cases where partners feel seriously troubled, they would do far better to seek professional guidance, either individually or as a couple, before undertaking a Summit.

ATTITUDE

The Summit is a lengthy and demanding experience. For most couples it will be a novel undertaking. Summit participants must be willing to approach this adventure with a positive attitude. They must believe they have the ability to direct the course of their lives. The willingness to work hard, to summon creative energy, and to persevere when things get difficult are part of the spirit partners must bring to the Summit.

Maintaining a realistic perspective is also essential. Partners are not going to solve all their problems in forty-eight hours, although they will probably get a good start. There will be negative as well as positive experiences as partners begin exploring new territory. The heart of the Summit is talking, plain and simple. Success is the responsibility of each couple and is directly proportional to the effort they make.

THE REWARDS

Couples reap immediate rewards from a successful Summit. The format supports equality and neutrality, enabling partners to talk openly about their concerns and come away with a deeper understanding of themselves, each other, and the relationship. They feel a sense of order and control in their lives because they have defined goals and discussed the roles they must assume to attain them. After the first Summit, a couple will have laid the groundwork for future growth based on the priorities they have identified. As they resume their daily activities, they can begin to make choices consistent with those plans.

The hours at a Summit can be among the most personal and intimate of the year. Devoting two days exclusively to themselves and their relationship helps a couple regain perspective about the special nature of their partnership. The Summit can be time of renewal, helping to reaffirm the bond between two people as friends, teammates, and lovers. Perhaps most important, a successful Summit provides a model for communication that a couple can continue to use throughout their lives. Over time and with practice, partners can integrate elements of the Summit process into their daily routines, to help them manage their relationship more effectively.

THE RISKS

Risk is inherent in any venture with the potential for great rewards, and the Summit process is no exception. Although engaging in the Summit process will not create problems in a relationship, it can highlight areas that are uncomfortable or even quite painful to deal with. In the process of honest dialogue, partners may find that their respective values, expectations, or goals are vastly different, perhaps even incompatible. In deciding to hold a Summit, a couple must accept the possibility that differences, large and small, will surface. As uncomfortable as this may be, admitting differences is the first step to understanding and resolving them.

Couples must also be willing to risk experiencing an unpredictable variety of emotions during a Summit. There is no telling what feelings might develop as you complete the Summit Exercises and talk about everything from the state of your finances to your love life. It is likely that those feelings will range all over the emotional map, from anxiety to excitement, anger to relief. Partners should be prepared for an intense experience, but should feel confident that the structure of the Summit process itself can help channel emotional responses into productive discussion.

Perhaps the greatest risk in undertaking a Summit is the risk of failure: having to acknowledge that, as partners, you are unable to communicate, negotiate conflict, or make mutually acceptable decisions. The possibility of failure is very real for couples who have never developed satisfactory ways of communicating or whose relationships are in trouble. However, it may be a risk worth taking. If you reach an impasse or are unable to make it through your Summit, you will have a strong signal to seek professional help. If you act on that signal, you are taking a positive step for your relationship. Far better to fail, admit it, and look for outside assistance than to allow the partnership to deteriorate beyond salvation.

IF YOU ARE READY . . .

If, after understanding the requirements and weighing the risks and rewards, you are ready to have your own Summit, read the next four chapters. They describe every step of the Summit process in detail.

PART TWO

THE SUMMIT PROCESS

CHAPTER **5**

THE PLANNING MEETING

Your Summit could well be one of the most important meetings you will ever attend. You must plan it with the same care and attention to detail you would employ when setting up an important business conference or organizing a special event. Stage One of the Summit process, the Planning Meeting, helps you get organized.

Planning takes place at a one- to two-hour session held well in advance of the Summit Meeting. The first task at this Planning Meeting is to amend and sign the Summit Contract, signifying your commitment to the Summit. Next, the logistics for the meeting are determined. You decide when and where to hold your Summit, what recreational and special activities to include, and how to handle meals. Finally, you develop an agenda for your Summit Talk.

☐ ☐ ☐

THE SUMMIT CONTRACT

The Summit Contract is an agreement between you, as partners, affirming your commitment to the spirit of the Summit process. It signifies your mutual pledge to invest the necessary resources and accept responsibility for the success of your Summit. A contract should be explicit, leaving nothing implied. The Summit Contract can be amended in any way to reflect your personal interpretation of the responsibilities and obligations involved in the Summit process.

SUMMIT CONTRACT

RESOLVED:

We are committed to engage in the Summit process as partners. We will take the time to plan our Summit Meeting and complete the Summit Exercises. We will reserve 48 consecutive hours for our Summit. Together we will share, explore, discuss, and resolve issues of concern. We will strive to maintain open and honest communication in an atmosphere of respect and trust. We will utilize our inner resources as individuals and our unique strength as a couple to improve communication, make mutually acceptable decisions, and plan for our future.

AMENDMENTS:

One week before our Summit we will tell each other how many more exercises we have left to do and, if necessary, spend Sunday morning newspaper time to complete them.

No matter how our Summit turns out, we will remember that we <u>both</u> decided to do this.

SIGNED: _Lynn Jarvis_   SIGNED: _Nick Schlopak_

DATE: _July 12_   DATE: _July 12_

SUMMIT LOGISTICS

There are several reasons for working out the details of your Summit Meeting in advance. First, by agreeing ahead of time about the type of activities and the time to be dedicated to them, you lessen the possibility of conflict over unfulfilled expectations or differences of opinion during your Summit. Second, deciding who is responsible for making the arrangements ensures that your Summit will indeed happen. Finally, the more coordination and preparation done in advance, the more time you will have to give to your talks. Think of the Summit as an important meeting, with very little room for spontaneity.

DATE

Picking a date for a Summit Meeting may not be as easy as it sounds. Remember, forty-eight consecutive hours must be allocated for the Summit. The date selected should be far enough in advance that you both have plenty of time in which to complete the Summit Exercises (these exercises require approximately five to eight hours of concentration). The Summit should be scheduled for a time that is devoid of major pressures or commitments other than the task at hand. For instance, December is probably not the best choice for a Summit Meeting given the nature of the season. Any time of year that typically requires extra hours at the office may also be a poor choice.

One important point to keep in mind: The Summit is *not* a vacation nor should it be planned as part of a vacation. The concentration and continuity needed requires that a Summit be a self-contained experience. One couple we know tried to devote two days of a week-long Hawaiian vacation to a Summit. It did not work; the beach was far too inviting, and on a sunny shore, sleep was preferable to sustained serious discussion.

PLACE

The surroundings can ultimately enhance or detract from the Summit experience, so the location should be selected with thought and care. The only cardinal rule: It must not be your own home. It can be hundreds of miles away or as close as a neighbor's apartment, but you should consider your home off-limits. There are several important reasons for insisting upon this restriction:

- A neutral setting seems to be far more conducive to productive discussion than an environment as emotionally charged as one's own home. Constructive discussion is more likely to take place away from the sources or reminders of conflict. Can two people hold a rational dialogue about the division of housework while surveying a stack of three-day-old dirty dishes? Is it possible for a couple to talk sensibly about their love life in the bed where they have recently had several misunderstandings about sex? In our experience the answer is an emphatic no.
- There are simply too many distractions around home to make serious, in-depth conversation possible for a sustained period. A ringing telephone, visiting neighbors, or crying children all serve to frustrate the kind of serious discussion that should take place at a Summit. And it is

just too easy to find diversions when the talk turns to difficult subjects. Running to the store, putting in a load of laundry, mowing the lawn, or watching an important football game can become convenient reasons for interrupting discussion when the going gets tough.

- Going away together is fun and something most couples do too infrequently. Stepping back from the daily routine helps partners regain a sense of their values and priorities. The romantic opportunities a new surrounding suggests add an important element of intimacy to the Summit experience.

In considering possible sites, partners should keep in mind the need for ample privacy. Conversation during the course of the meeting will range over highly personal and sensitive ground. Select a spot where you can talk openly, cry, hug, or yell if you want to; a place where you will not be inhibited by scores of strangers or distracted by frenetic activity or constant noise.

Think, too, about comfort. You will be sitting for long periods of time, so your surroundings should be pleasant and not too confining. It's nice to have enough space to spread out the Summit Exercises and notes and to sprawl comfortably— a stuffy, cramped room is not particularly conducive to long hours of dialogue. There may well be times during the two days when you feel the need to spend a few moments by yourself to reflect or just take a break from your partner. It helps to have different areas, indoors or out, to move to alone or together.

Consider the recreational opportunities available. Although the majority of the Summit will be spent in dialogue, there will be some hours for relaxation and recreation. Take that opportunity to do something you enjoy. However, be aware that an abundance of recreational possibilities might lure you from the main purpose of the Summit—talking. If you think the slopes would be an overwhelming temptation, do not hold your Summit at a ski resort. Remember, this is a working holiday.

Think about travel time. You do not want to spend too much time in transit or arrive at your Summit site feeling exhausted from a long drive. Finally, of course, you must consider your budget. How much can you afford, or are you willing to spend, on this experience? The possibilities for Summit sites are limited only by your imagination. Some possible Summit sites are:

a country inn

a tent in the mountains

a friend's house (trade yours for the weekend)

a resort

a rented camper

your parents' vacation home

a lakeside cabin

a city hotel.

RECREATION

Recreational time not only makes the two days more enjoyable but also periodically allows partners to relax and rejuvenate so they can make the most of their Summit discussions. Physical exercise, such as running, walking, cross-country skiing, biking, swimming, or tennis, can help relieve the mental fatigue that comes from hours of intense and concentrated discussion. Quieter activities, such as a nap in the sun, a sauna, or a stroll in the woods, also offer an antidote to mental and emotional exhaustion. The recreational activities you select should make you feel good and leave you feeling relaxed.

SPECIAL ACTIVITIES

In the course of busy lives, partners often forget or don't make time to do the little things that encourage intimacy or show how much they really care for each other. Special activities at the Summit give each partner a chance to do something out of the ordinary for, or with, the other. These experiences can balance the more cerebral and emotionally stressful activities of the Summit.

The variety of special activities is limitless and the choice is obviously very personal. Some suggestions are:

renew marriage vows

give each other a massage

read a special poem to each other

exchange gifts

dress up (or down)

give each other a bath and shampoo

celebrate an anniversary.

MEALS

Taking into account the facilities available at your Summit site, you will have to decide whether to prepare your own meals or dine out. If you will be doing some of your own cooking, it's a good idea to get your grocery shopping done before you begin. You don't want to take time away from your Summit to walk the aisles of a supermarket . . . or worse, discover that you cannot buy groceries anywhere nearby.

SUMMIT LOGISTICS PLANNER

The Summit Logistics Planner has a place to indicate the date and place of your Summit. You also fill in information about recreation, special activities, meals, and travel. Once you arrive at your site, this planner, along with your Summit Talk Agenda, is used to develop the Summit Timetable—a detailed account of the hours at your Summit.

SUMMIT LOGISTICS PLANNER

SUMMIT MEETING   DATE   SITE

1ST CHOICE   Feb. 14-16   Jan & Tom's Cabin

2ND CHOICE   March 8-10   Glen Oak Inn

PERSON IN CHARGE OF MAKING SITE ARRANGEMENTS   Emily

RECREATIONAL ACTIVITIES

3-4 mile run (cabin or inn)
x-c skiing (cabin)
squash (inn)
sauna

SPECIAL ACTIVITIES

celebrate 1st meeting with
champagne (like we had then)
make blueberry pancakes
    (cabin)
dinner at Chez Jacqueline
    (inn)
read poem to each other

MEALS

MEALS	WHERE	TIME
dinner	fast food	½ hr.
breakfast	cabin (inn)	½ hr.
lunch	picnic	1½ hr
dinner	cabin	
	(Chez Jacqueline)	2½ hr.
breakfast	cabin (inn)	½ hr.
lunch	see how things go.	on way home?

PERSON RESPONSIBLE FOR GROCERY
SHOPPING PRIOR TO DEPARTURE
    Tuck

TRANSPORTATION MODE

car

PERSON RESPONSIBLE FOR
TRANSPORTATION ARRANGEMENTS
    Emily (gas, chains)

TRAVEL TIME
    2½ hrs. (cabin)
    45 min. (inn)

THE SUMMIT TALK AGENDA

Managers know that a good agenda helps make meetings productive. An agenda outlines the various items for discussion so participants can organize their ideas, budget their time, and keep the meeting on track. The Summit Talk Agenda serves a similar purpose.

Developing the Summit Talk Agenda in advance of the Summit Meeting accomplishes several things. First, both partners know what subjects will be discussed, thereby alleviating some anxiety over potential surprises. Second, both partners can collect their thoughts, organize their ideas, and get emotionally prepared for discussion about the range of topics they have identified. Finally, the agenda provides a detailed guide to the talks, which enables partners to use their time wisely.

SUMMIT TALK PHASES

Summit Talk comprises three distinct phases. The Summit Talk Agenda (see page 54) provides a framework for discussion during each phase. To facilitate the first Summit, portions of the agenda have been filled in with mandatory tasks—activities that we and friends have found to be essential to a smooth Summit. At your Planning Meeting you personalize the balance of the agenda to reflect your specific interests.

THE THREE PHASES OF SUMMIT TALK

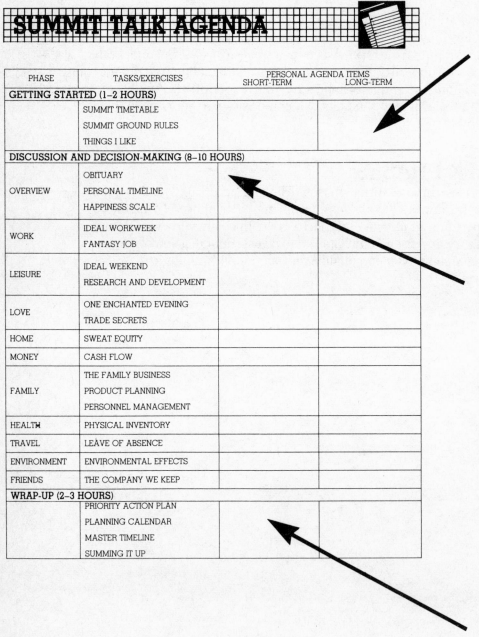

SUMMIT TALK AGENDA

PHASE	TASKS/EXERCISES	PERSONAL AGENDA ITEMS	
		SHORT-TERM	LONG-TERM
GETTING STARTED (1–2 HOURS)			
	SUMMIT TIMETABLE		
	SUMMIT GROUND RULES		
	THINGS I LIKE		
DISCUSSION AND DECISION-MAKING (8–10 HOURS)			
OVERVIEW	OBITUARY		
	PERSONAL TIMELINE		
	HAPPINESS SCALE		
WORK	IDEAL WORKWEEK		
	FANTASY JOB		
LEISURE	IDEAL WEEKEND		
	RESEARCH AND DEVELOPMENT		
LOVE	ONE ENCHANTED EVENING		
	TRADE SECRETS		
HOME	SWEAT EQUITY		
MONEY	CASH FLOW		
FAMILY	THE FAMILY BUSINESS		
	PRODUCT PLANNING		
	PERSONNEL MANAGEMENT		
HEALTH	PHYSICAL INVENTORY		
TRAVEL	LEAVE OF ABSENCE		
ENVIRONMENT	ENVIRONMENTAL EFFECTS		
FRIENDS	THE COMPANY WE KEEP		
WRAP-UP (2–3 HOURS)			
	PRIORITY ACTION PLAN		
	PLANNING CALENDAR		
	MASTER TIMELINE		
	SUMMING IT UP		

Getting Started consists of a series of tasks and exercises designed to ease partners into their Summit Talk. These tasks will take about an hour and should be done in the order outlined.

Discussion and Decision-Making is the body of the talks. During this phase, partners share and discuss their Summit Exercises. Partners also talk about personal issues of interest or concern that they have identified. Discussion in this phase is organized around the ten functional areas. Discussion Guidelines provide ideas for addressing specific issues. Decisions and commitments are recorded on Action Plans. This phase takes about ten hours.

Wrap-Up gives partners a chance to summarize their experience and translate their ideas and decisions into plans they can implement at home. This final phase requires one to two hours.

SUMMIT TALK AGENDA

PHASE	TASKS/EXERCISES	PERSONAL AGENDA ITEMS SHORT-TERM	LONG-TERM
GETTING STARTED (1–2 HOURS)			
	SUMMIT TIMETABLE		
	SUMMIT GROUND RULES		
	THINGS I LIKE		
DISCUSSION AND DECISION-MAKING (8–10 HOURS)			
OVERVIEW	OBITUARY		
	PERSONAL TIMELINE		
	HAPPINESS SCALE		
WORK	IDEAL WORKWEEK		
	FANTASY JOB		
LEISURE	IDEAL WEEKEND		
	RESEARCH AND DEVELOPMENT		
LOVE	ONE ENCHANTED EVENING		
	TRADE SECRETS		
HOME	SWEAT EQUITY		
MONEY	CASH FLOW		
FAMILY	THE FAMILY BUSINESS		
	PRODUCT PLANNING		
	PERSONNEL MANAGEMENT		
HEALTH	PHYSICAL INVENTORY		
TRAVEL	LEAVE OF ABSENCE		
ENVIRONMENT	ENVIRONMENTAL EFFECTS		
FRIENDS	THE COMPANY WE KEEP		
WRAP-UP (2–3 HOURS)			
	PRIORITY ACTION PLAN		
	PLANNING CALENDAR		
	MASTER TIMELINE		
	SUMMING IT UP		

THE FUNCTIONAL AREAS

At the Planning Meeting, partners complete their Summit Talk Agenda by determining the personal agenda items they want to address in the Discussion and Decision-Making phase. The ten functional areas of a partnership provide an organizing concept for developing this part of the agenda. Remember, functional areas are the broad categories of the life of the contemporary couple. Thinking in terms of these functional areas makes it easier to sort out problems and conflicts that must be resolved and define issues that must be addressed. Although many personal agenda items are interrelated, any topic a partner wants to discuss should fit, at least roughly, into one of the following ten functional areas:

WORK: This term describes any area of activity that has economic significance to the partnership whether or not it results in a paycheck. In addition to the activities traditionally considered "work," this definition includes housekeeping, child-rearing, and managing the social life of the partnership.

LEISURE: This category includes all activities outside of work in which partners engage and from which they gain personal satisfaction. It embraces recreational, social, cultural, philanthropic, athletic, political, and religious pursuits.

LOVE: This is the realm of emotional, physical, intellectual, and spiritual connections between two people.

HOME: This area comprises the range of day-to-day domestic activities from housework to cooking to laundry to walking the dog. It also includes topics of long-range concern, such as major home repair, maintenance, or renovation.

MONEY: This functional area includes all the practical issues about making, saving, and spending dollars. It also embraces the more subtle issues of power and authority as they relate to money matters in the partnership.

FAMILY: This category deals with relations between and among immediate and extended family members, including parents, in-laws, children, and siblings.

HEALTH: This area deals with the physical, mental, emotional, and intellectual well-being of each partner.

TRAVEL: This could be considered a subset of Leisure, but it is given its own heading to distinguish travel-related activities from day-to-day leisure-time activities. It embraces vacations, exotic adventures, weekend jaunts, or trips of any length that require forethought and planning.

ENVIRONMENT: This category covers issues about where to live, including type of dwelling, neighborhood, community, and geographic area.

FRIENDS: This functional area deals with relations with anyone from best buddies to business acquaintances.

DEVELOPING THE AGENDA

The first step in developing the agenda is to brainstorm about all the possible topics you want to discuss at your Summit. What might be included? Anything, absolutely anything either partner feels the need to talk about should be included. Those ideas should be noted on the Summit Agenda Planner in the most appropriate functional area. If it is an issue of long-term concern (beyond the coming year) list it in that column. If it is a topic of short-term concern (within the coming year) put it under that heading. The sample Summit Agenda Planner on page 52 illustrates the range and variety of personal agenda items a couple might include.

SUMMIT AGENDA PLANNER

FUNCTIONAL AREA	PERSONAL AGENDA ITEMS	
	SHORT-TERM	LONG-TERM
WORK	Bart's time at office Ph.D. programs for Beth	own practice—when? how? how grad. school fits with family responsibilities?
LEISURE	bridge group volunteer work start flute – when? ballet subscription – cost?	adventure activities public service
LOVE	sex life	time away from it all
HOME	mess! new dishwasher hot tub?	kitchen renovation
MONEY	magazine subscriptions budget IRAs	buy boat - when?
FAMILY	help with Lauren & Jamie holidays – how spend? decide about school for girls	music lessons for girls care for Dad adopt boy?
HEALTH	exhaustion – real problem join health club therapy	get girls involved in regular exercise
TRAVEL	Joel & Susan's wedding weekend canoe trip - summer	exotic travel Japan for convention next year
ENVIRONMENT	house size	move back to west coast
FRIENDS	getting together with friends from work how to stay in touch with city friends.	regular reunions with friends from California til we get back.

When partners are finished brainstorming about discussion topics, they transfer the notes from the Summit Agenda Planner to the Summit Talk Agenda (see page 54). The final agenda shows all tasks, exercises, and personal items to be discussed at the Summit and will guide participants through their Summit Talk.

SUMMIT TALK AGENDA

PHASE	TASKS/EXERCISES	PERSONAL AGENDA ITEMS SHORT-TERM	LONG-TERM
GETTING STARTED (1–2 HOURS)			
	SUMMIT TIMETABLE		
	SUMMIT GROUND RULES		
	THINGS I LIKE		
DISCUSSION AND DECISION-MAKING (8–10 HOURS)			
OVERVIEW	OBITUARY		
	PERSONAL TIMELINE		
	HAPPINESS SCALE		
WORK	IDEAL WORKWEEK	Bart - office time	own practice
	FANTASY JOB	Beth - Ph.d ———————→	
LEISURE	IDEAL WEEKEND	volunteer work music / ballet	adventure activities
	RESEARCH AND DEVELOPMENT	friends	public service
LOVE	ONE ENCHANTED EVENING	sex	time away
	TRADE SECRETS		
HOME	SWEAT EQUITY	mess	kitchen
MONEY	CASH FLOW	budget / investments	boat
FAMILY	THE FAMILY BUSINESS	holidays	3rd child
	PRODUCT PLANNING		
	PERSONNEL MANAGEMENT	competition between twins	
HEALTH	PHYSICAL INVENTORY	health club counseling	exercise for girls
TRAVEL	LEAVE OF ABSENCE	wedding canoe trip	Japan
ENVIRONMENT	ENVIRONMENTAL EFFECTS	house	move
FRIENDS	THE COMPANY WE KEEP	work friends city friends	California friends
WRAP-UP (2–3 HOURS)			
	PRIORITY ACTION PLAN		
	PLANNING CALENDAR		
	MASTER TIMELINE		
	SUMMING IT UP		

After the Planning Meeting, partners will have a good idea about the scope of their upcoming Summit. The agenda can be posted in a place where it is easily seen. Any other discussion topics that come to mind can be added to the agenda. In the meantime, partners will prepare for their talks by completing the Summit Exercises.

CHAPTER 6

THE SUMMIT EXERCISES

WHAT ARE THE SUMMIT EXERCISES?

Prior to leaving for the Summit Meeting, each partner will complete the Summit Exercises—eighteen in all—which act as a catalyst for discussion of each functional area during the Summit Talk. The exercises come in a variety of shapes and forms. Some are scales, others graphs; still others resemble report cards. Some ask for short-answer responses; others ask for mini-essays. Some focus on issues of immediate concern; others look to the future. Some of the exercises ask partners to assess their satisfaction with various aspects of their life. Others are designed to help clarify values and priorities and to explore expectations. All raise provocative questions designed to educe information that partners can use to manage their relationship. The chart on page 57 shows what the Summit Exercises might reveal.

Each of the Summit Exercises relates primarily to one of the ten functional areas of a partnership. But because all the functional areas are interrelated, one exercise may address issues in several areas. The illustration on page 58 shows the major focus of each exercise.

WHAT DO THEY DO?

As the core of the Summit Talk the exercises serve a number of purposes. They stimulate thinking about a variety of issues including roles and goals in the partnership. In conjunction with the Discussion Guidelines and Action Plans, they facilitate communication at the Summit and support shared decision-making. They assist in addressing complex issues in an organized fashion, thereby helping make the Summit a productive experience for the participants. The Summit Exercises help couples begin to integrate the attributes of good management into their partnership while their Summit is in progress.

GOALS

A number of the Summit Exercises are specifically designed to help partners identify long-term goals. Although most of the exercises ask very basic questions, their unusual format stimulates creativity and reduces inhibitions. For example, many of the exercises give participants license to play with their ideas and dreams, to indulge in fantasy, to create an ideal situation. By game playing in this way, partners begin to clarify essential values that can make setting long-term goals easier.

Other exercises help partners establish shorter-term objectives for everything from child-rearing to domestic chores. These exercises ask partners to rate their current level of satisfaction, identify desired objectives, and to think about ways to achieve them. By the end of their Summit Talk, partners should have a clear sense of priorities for the coming twelve months, as well as strategies to accomplish their goals.

ROLES

Because gender no longer dictates the rules, a couple must determine the roles each partner will play in their relationship. Several Summit Exercises give part-

WHAT THE SUMMIT EXERCISES REVEAL

EXERCISES	CURRENT SATISFACTION	GOALS/OBJECTIVES		ROLES/RESPONSIBILITIES	VALUES/PRIORITIES
		Short-Term	Long-Term		
OBITUARY			•		•
PERSONAL TIMELINE			•		•
HAPPINESS SCALE	•				
IDEAL WORKWEEK		•			•
FANTASY JOB			•		•
IDEAL WEEKEND		•	•	•	•
RESEARCH AND DEVELOPMENT		•			•
ONE ENCHANTED EVENING					•
TRADE SECRETS	•	•		•	
SWEAT EQUITY	•	•	•	•	
CASH FLOW	•	•	•		•
THE FAMILY BUSINESS		•		•	
PRODUCT PLANNING			•	•	
PERSONNEL MANAGEMENT	•	•	•	•	•
PHYSICAL INVENTORY	•	•			
LEAVE OF ABSENCE		•	•		•
ENVIRONMENTAL EFFECTS			•		•
THE COMPANY WE KEEP		•		•	•

ners the opportunity to explore the interdependent roles that keep their relationship healthy, and assess their satisfaction with them. Some exercises ask about individual needs and interests so that partners might better understand each other's role expectations. A few exercises ask partners to articulate values and priorities. Comparing responses gives them a chance to see how their respective roles influence their outlook on a particular issue.

SHARED DECISION-MAKING

Consensus, or shared decision-making, is a process that takes into account the views of all parties affected by a particular decision. Throughout their Summit, a couple will be making decisions that affect them for the coming year and into the future. The Summit Exercises give couples the opportunity to share, listen, discuss, and debate in a way that can lead to mutually acceptable choices. The exercises help partners communicate their needs, priorities, interests, and values by expediting the exchange of information necessary for negotiating agreement. The Discussion Guidelines accompanying the exercises support shared decision-making by encouraging couples to create Action Plans that reflect consensus.

COMMUNICATION

The Summit Exercises support communication in several ways. First, the exercises give partners a common basis for beginning their Summit Talk. Because both partners complete the same Summit Exercises, they have a shared experience upon which to build their talks.

FUNCTIONAL AREAS/SUMMIT EXERCISES

	OBITUARY	TIMELINE	HAPPINESS SCALE	IDEAL WORKWEEK	FANTASY JOB	IDEAL WEEKEND	RESEARCH AND DEVELOPMENT	ONE ENCHANTED EVENING	TRADE SECRETS	SWEAT EQUITY	CASH FLOW	THE FAMILY BUSINESS	PRODUCT PLANNING	PERSONNEL MANAGEMENT	PHYSICAL INVENTORY	LEAVE OF ABSENCE	ENVIRONMENTAL EFFECTS	THE COMPANY WE KEEP
WORK	√	√	√	√	√													
LEISURE	√	√	√	√	√	√	√											
LOVE	√	√	√					√	√									
HOME	√	√	√							√								
MONEY	√	√	√								√							
FAMILY	√	√	√									√	√	√				
HEALTH	√	√	√												√			
TRAVEL	√	√	√													√		
ENVIRONMENT	√	√	√														√	
FRIENDS	√	√	√															√

Second, the exercises help partners focus their thinking about topics that may be overwhelming. The exercises bring structure to the issues. At the Summit, the exercises provide an organizing framework that helps the Summit Talk flow logically and efficiently.

Third, the exercises help partners share thoughts and feelings they may hesitate expressing directly to one another. Responding to a question on a piece of paper first makes it easier to talk about sensitive subjects. Some of the exercises allow partners to write descriptions, make lists, or develop charts as a way to send a message. Each exercise provides a unique way to get important information out in the open.

QUALITY TIME

The Summit Exercises can be the basis for a meaningful exchange of ideas and a satisfying resolution of conflict. Moreover, they are great fun to share and discuss. But most importantly, the information elicited by the exercises can help a couple devise ways to incorporate quality-time experiences into their lives on a regular basis.

USING THE EXERCISES

The Summit Exercises are an integral part of the Summit Talk. Partners begin discussion of each functional area on the agenda by sharing their responses to the related Summit Exercise(s). Discussion Guidelines for each functional area offer suggestions for addressing the issues raised by the exercises. While the exercises are valuable in and of themselves, they should also be used as background data for addressing the personal agenda items partners have noted.

COMPLETING THE SUMMIT EXERCISES

Well in advance of the Summit Meeting, each partner should independently complete his or her set of exercises. Because the Summit Exercises require concentration, they should be completed alone in a quiet spot, away from the distractions of work, children, and the telephone. Plan to spend approximately five to eight hours on the exercises.

As you work on your Summit Exercises remember there are no right or wrong answers. This is not a test. The challenge is to respond as thoughtfully and honestly as you can. Each exercise includes specific instructions for its completion. Work on the exercises in any order you wish, although you might want to save the Personal Timeline until last, as a summary exercise. Feel free to outline your thoughts before filling in the exercises, make notes, use additional sheets of paper, or expand your responses in any way, shape, or form.

Some of the exercises will be exciting and stimulating. Others may be intimidating or disconcerting. A few will appear simplistic or tedious. Don't reject them. Take the time to work through all the exercises as best you can. Fruitful and interesting discussions will result from the most unexpected sources. Your effort will pay off. If you do get stuck on a particular exercise, for whatever reason, put it aside and come back to it later. But, by the time you depart for your Summit Meeting, all exercises should be completed.

SAMPLE SUMMIT EXERCISES

By now you are probably curious about the exercises themselves. To give you a better understanding of them, examples are presented next, grouped under their respective functional area. These examples are based on completed exercises that friends shared with us and reflect a range of personal experiences and approaches.

OVERVIEW

These exercises are designed to give you the "big picture" of your life. Obituary asks you to assume a retrospective attitude about your life and accomplishments. (This exercise was inspired by the article "Life Planning" in the book *The Planning of Change*, edited by Bennis, Benne, Chin, and Corey.) Personal Timeline asks you to look ahead from the vantage point of where you are now in order to establish some objectives. Happiness Scale asks you to assess your satisfaction with various facets of your life currently. These exercises provide the background for more detailed discussion of the various functional areas and will be used throughout your Summit Talk.

Peter Hanson passed away at the age of 82. The cause of death was heart failure. Mr. Hanson had led a very full life. He is best known for his business success, having risen to the top of a major manufacturing concern by the age of 42. To his colleagues' surprise and his family's delight, he abandoned his comfortable position after only three years, to found a hugely successful company to produce solar shingles, now a standard element of housing construction. Mr. Hanson's invention revealed a less-recognized aspect of his talents. Although without any formal technical training, he harbored a curiosity and creative ability that won him eight patents.

Mr. Hanson is reported to have been an accomplished climber, photographer and clarinetist, activities he took up only in his middle years. His artistic and outdoor talents grew out of Mr. Hanson's often stated desire to be a modern Renaissance man. The standards against which he measured himself were revealed when, in response to a reporter's comment that he must be very satisfied with having such a wide variety of accomplishments, he said, "Are you kidding? Look at Da Vinci. That was a human being!"

During his later years Peter Hanson was a figure in political circles, as he followed his wife Patricia Marlis-Hanson to Washington, where she served in Congress for six years. Following their retirement and the acquisition of Nite and Day Shingles, Mr. Hanson and his wife of over 50 years relocated to the Lake Tahoe region. The seasonal tourist trade at their antique store enabled them to travel widely.

Mr. Hanson is survived by his wife Patricia, 79, a daughter Bonnie, and son, Clyde.

PERSONAL TIMELINE

YEAR OR AGE	(35) 85 86 87 88 89 90 91 92 93 94 95	(50) 2000	(55) 2005	(60) 2010	(65) 2015	(70) 2020
WORK	BUSINESS NEW VENTURES	GRAD SCHOOL PUBLIC POLICY / GOV'T	TEACH	FOUNDATION WORK	BOARDS OF DIRECTORS / TRAVEL	
LEISURE	TENNIS, TENNIS, TENNIS					
LOVE	LOTS OF ROMANTIC EXPERIENCES!	25TH ANNIVERSARY!				
HOME	FIRST HOME	SECOND HOME (VACATION)		N.Y.C. APARTMENT		
MONEY	$100K–200K SALARY / $1–5 MILLION CAPITAL GAINS	Ø	50K	40K	Ø	75K
FAMILY	FIRST CHILD	SECOND CHILD		FAMILIES SEVERAL TIMES/YEAR		
HEALTH	ALWAYS RUN, BIKE, SWIM VEGETARIAN DIET					
TRAVEL	EUROPE ASIA			LOTS OF INTERNATIONAL TRAVEL		
ENVIRONMENT	"SILICON VALLEY"	BOSTON CAMBRIDGE	J.D. NEW ENGLAND	N.Y.C.	LIVE ON WEST COAST / APT. IN N.Y.C.	
FRIENDS	CULTIVATE LASTING FRIENDSHIPS					

	WORK	LEISURE	LOVE	HOME	MONEY	HEALTH	TRAVEL	ENVIRONMENT	FRIENDS	FAMILY
10										
9										
8										
7	7					7		8½	7	7½
6			6		6½					
5				5½						
4		4½								
3										
2							2½			
1										

WORK

These exercises help you address issues related to your job and career. Ideal Workweek asks you to envision the perfect week for you today; this will help you better understand how improvements in your current schedule might lead to greater satisfaction. Fantasy Job gives you a chance to indulge your secret fantasies about a job experience, helping you identify characteristics that you might seek in a real position.

TIME	MONDAY	TUESDAY	WEDNESDAY	THURSDAY	FRIDAY
M O R N I N G	8am. to office meetings with associates meeting with clients	6:30 squash breakfast at desk desk work review assoc.'s reports.	make breakfast for family late to office desk work	6:30 squash breakfast at club 8:00 work on proposals review project status	run 6-7 miles teach class at university
A F T E R N O O N	12 - light work out lunch at desk desk work ↓ late	lunch with univ. V.P. meeting to present new project early home	lunch with associates visit other offices 5:00 - swim	lunch at desk expenses professional journals phone calls work late	lunch with students. research at university early home
E V E N I N G	dinner without kids read music	dinner with kids play/read to them early bed	dinner in town with friends late bed	7:30 dinner home late night walk with Veronica	

FANTASY JOB

POSITION: _Creative Vice President_

RESPONSIBILITIES/DUTIES: _Creative director for development of innovative children's educational toys. Spend time with children's focus and play groups in U.S. and abroad. Design new toys. Talk about and display them on T.V., trade shows, etc._

AGE: _37_

LOCATION: _Portland_

HIGHLIGHTS/ACCOMPLISHMENTS: _____
1. created new magazine for parents and children
2. $1 million in sales of new toys
3. sponsored summer exchange visits for 8-12-year-olds.

NOTES: _Worked with my family_
spent 30% of time overseas.

LEISURE

These exercises give you a chance to define priorities for your free time. Ideal Weekend asks you to describe your perfect weekend. Comparing responses helps you spot areas of potential conflict or disagreement in your partnership so you can make adjustments to better fulfill your individual needs and each other's expectations. Research and Development helps you establish some goals and priorities for your free time, both alone and together.

IDEAL WEEKEND

	FRIDAY	SATURDAY	SUNDAY
6:00 A.M.		exercise class or run 3-5 miles	exercise class or run
7:00 A.M.			
8:00 A.M.			
9:00 A.M.		Errands gardening reading	coffee with new York Times
10:00 A.M.			
11:00 A.M.			
12:00 P.M.			
1:00 P.M.			
2:00 P.M.		Tennis w/ friends	Beach or Bike ride or Sail or Hike
3:00 P.M.			
4:00 P.M.		make love, nap	
5:00 P.M.			
6:00 P.M.	exercise class	Dinner with friends, out or at home or Theater or Dancing or Party	Dinner at home
7:00 P.M.			
8:00 P.M.	movie		
9:00 P.M.			Read/TV
10:00 P.M.	burgers & beer		
11:00 P.M.	11:30 — bed!		☆Go away for weekend at least once every 6 weeks
12:00 A.M.			
1:00 A.M.			
2:00 A.M.			

	LEISURE ACTIVITIES	WHEN/HOW OFTEN	MINE	OURS
T H I S Y E A R	Harp lessons	once a week	✓	
	swim	every morning	✓	
	Philharmonic season Tickets	once a month		✓
	photography / darkroom	whenever possible	✓	
	vegetable garden	spring		✓
	volunteer senior home	once a month		✓

	LEISURE ACTIVITIES	WHEN/HOW OFTEN	MINE	OURS
F U T U R E	play in community orchestra	in 5 years	✓	
	start book discussion group	next year		✓
	formal dinner party for friends	twice a year		✓
	triathlon	next year ?	✓	

LOVE

These exercises help you address one of the more difficult subjects to talk about. One Enchanted Evening asks you to invent the most romantic experience you can imagine, which will likely stimulate more romance in your relationship. Trade Secrets gives each of you the opportunity to reveal your thoughts about ways your love life might be improved.

MY ENCHANTED EVENING WOULD BEGIN ABOUT _4_ O'CLOCK

We'd be vacationing at a private cottage on some tropical island. You'd be wearing an evening dress and I'd have on a tux. We'd walk the short way to the dock where a sloop would be awaiting our arrival. The warm breeze would carry us across the bay to a deserted shore, and we'd have a dinner of fresh fish prepared on board by the chef, with a favorite fine wine and raspberries for dessert. Classical music would drift back over the water from the string quartet on the dock.

After dinner the sloop would leave us ashore to walk to an undiscovered night club, where we would dance to the beat of a local band. After an hour or so, we return to the boat and sail back to our island, the moon an iridescent globe just above the horizon. As the stars appeared and the sloop disappeared over the dark water we would start a languorous walk to the cottage. As we cross the warm sand, we stop and exchange mischievous smiles. Your gown and my tux fall to the beach. We race, laughing, to the warm water. The water is soothing, the night and you are lovely.

At the cottage we dry each other off after a quick shower. I pour us a glass of liqueur which we sip between cuddles in bed. Finally we make love and drift off to sleep, just as the morning light breaks.

TRADE SECRETS

	SEX	ROMANCE
FIVE THINGS I WOULD LIKE YOU TO DO MORE OFTEN	1. sleep without your cares! 2. take the initiative 3. reverse positions / make some change 4. invite me into the tub 5. make love more often	give me back rubs read poetry to me play the piano for me watch me coach the soccer team wear your hair down
FIVE THINGS I THINK YOU WOULD LIKE ME TO DO MORE OFTEN	1. stay awake and talk afterwards 2. hug you more 3. be gentler 4. kiss you more 5. more foreplay	hold hands with you compliment you more often go shopping with you write you notes call you at the office
FIVE THINGS I WOULD LIKE TO DO ALONE WITH YOU MORE OFTEN	1. take walks 2. work out 3. go to soccer games 4. go out to breakfast 5. go dancing	

HOME

The exercise for this area, Sweat Equity, focuses on the state of the home. It asks you to assess your satisfaction with the current division of domestic responsibility and suggest ways that it might be improved. It also asks you to identify priorities for larger home-related projects. Deciding who does what and establishing priorities for this area can help put you on track to accomplish projects that never seem to get done.

SWEAT EQUITY

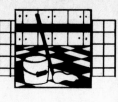

TASK	WHO DOES	RATING (1-5) TODAY	FUTURE	HOW TO ACHIEVE
House cleaning	E - 80% C - 20%			
vacuum		1	5	⎫ HIRE A
dusting		1	5	⎬ HOUSEKEEPER
bathrooms		1	5	⎬ 1 DAY
floors		1	5	⎭ A WEEK
Grocery shopping	E	3	4	should pick regular time to shop
Fix dinner	E	5	5	works out fine
wash dishes	C	5	5	great — as long as you do them!
Laundry	E	2	2	I hate it - but I'll do it
Drycleaning shirts	E - 50% C - 50%	3	5	you do it all — more convenient for you
social calendar	E	5	5	I like it
Bill paying,				you need to do it more often
checkbook	C	3	5	
Pet care	C	5	5	you are great thank you!

PET PEEVES

* sweaty running clothes on bed
* hair in shower drain
* uncovered food in fridge
* overflowing garbage cans

HOME PROJECTS

THIS YEAR

WHAT	WHEN
Pull up rugs	
Redo floors	by Fall
replace shower head	next week
Frame posters	by end of month

FUTURE

WHAT	WHEN
Remodel bathroom	next year
build bookshelves in study	next year
move to larger place	3-5 years

MONEY

Cash Flow gives you the opportunity to explore several different aspects of the financial situation in your partnership. Clarifying your thoughts and devising mutually acceptable guidelines for managing your finances can help minimize tension in this area.

CASH FLOW

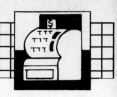

RATE YOUR SATISFACTION WITH:	1	2	3	4	5	WHAT WOULD YOU CHANGE?
INCOME			X			*wish you would go back to work at least part-time*
THE WAY SPENDING DECISIONS ARE MADE		X				*I don't get to back decisions because we never have enough $ after paying bills*
SAVINGS AND INVESTMENTS	X					*more time to follow market* *Add $1500 to trust each year*

PET PEEVES ABOUT MONEY

you want nice things but I pay for them what about me? I never see a dime

Paying for your wardrobe

MAJOR PURCHASES I WOULD LIKE TO MAKE

THIS YEAR	NEXT 5 YEARS
new car $14,000	trip to
join down town	Hawaii
athletic club $5,000	new ski
video recorder $1,000	equipment

PERCENTAGE OF JOINT INCOME SPENT ON:

RENT/MORTGAGE	35
DINING OUT	3
GROCERIES	5
CLOTHING (ME)	.5
CLOTHING (YOU)	2
CHILD CARE	2
DOMESTIC HELP	—
RECREATION	3
TRAVEL/VACATIONS	2.5
UTILITIES/PHONE	1.5
TRANSPORTATION/CAR	2
PERSONAL CARE (ME)	1
PERSONAL CARE (YOU)	1.5
MEDICAL/DENTAL	.5
PSYCHOLOGICAL	—
LOAN REPAYMENT/ INTEREST	5
LEGAL/TAX/FINANCIAL	30
?	5.5
	= 100%

HOW DO YOU FEEL ABOUT YOUR CURRENT BUDGET? *This is a great idea -but we should have real numbers! start a written budget.*

FAMILY

The series of exercises in this area deal with issues of parenting and relations with members of the extended family. The Family Business asks you to define and delegate responsibility for fulfilling obligations to relatives in order to avoid conflict. Product Planning gives those who are considering parenthood a chance to explore role expectations as a way to better understand the changes that follow the birth of a child. Personnel Management gives parents a chance to assess their satisfaction with their roles, identify problem areas and goals for their children, and explore how parenting affects their relationship with one another.

FAMILY MEMBER	ACTION	PERSON RESPONSIBLE
mum	B-Day present Dinner with 2x month	me
pop	B-Day present invite to watch basketball games	me
Donna, Michael, Kids	call once a month	me
Aunt Sarah	visit at home once a month	you
Uncle Dean	dinner/bowling 4 times a year	you
Gran	lunch & shopping once every 2 months B-Day card, holiday cards	me
Nana	send card every 2 weeks & postcards from anywhere	you
Mom & Dad	B-Day & Holiday cards call once/week, send photos regularly	you
K.B.	visit 2 times a year, call once a month	me
Sally & Jeff	call at college once a month, write occasionally	you

TIME TO BE SPENT WITH FAMILY MEMBERS THIS YEAR		
WHO	WHEN	WHERE
Mom & Dad Nana	Thanksgiving	St. Paul
Gran	Spring / Easter ?	San Antonio
Sally & Jeff	July	Des Moines (Tommy's wedding)
K.B.	April	Santa Barbara
Mum & Pop	Christmas	here (at our house this year!)

JOT DOWN ANY THOUGHTS YOU WANT TO DISCUSS
RELATED TO THIS TOPIC

DO YOU WANT TO HAVE
CHILDREN?   **NO**

YES

WHAT CHANGES DO
YOU THINK WILL OCCUR
IN YOUR LIFE?

1. less time with friends
2. fewer discretionary $"
3. feel closer to Joan

HOW DO YOU
FEEL ABOUT THAT?

1. don't want to lose friends
2. scares me
3. can't wait

YOU	YOUR PARTNER
teacher	nurturer
coach	cleaner
listener	teacher
judge	"mom"
friend	

WHAT ROLES DO
YOU EXPECT TO
PLAY IN RAISING
YOUR CHILDREN?

WHAT FACTORS WILL
INFLUENCE YOUR
DECISION ABOUT THE
TIMING AND SPACING
OF CHILDREN?

financial security
home situation (enough space?)
feeling "ready"
have gone on our adventure

HOW MANY CHILDREN
WOULD YOU LIKE TO HAVE?
WHEN?

2
1988, 1991

OTHER ISSUES

my childhood
Joan's mom

PERSONNEL MANAGEMENT

TASK	PERSON RESPONSIBLE	SATIS-FACTION (1-5)	POSSIBLE SATIS-FACTION (1-5)	HOW
Get Avery up/dressed	M	2	5	you take over that job
Fix breakfast	M	4	4	no changes
supervise breakfast	M/Y	3	5	you were more interactive w/ Avery
pack Avery's lunch	M	3	3	I'll never like it
drop Avery at school	M	1	5	you do it
pick Avery up from school	M	5	5	I love to see her at end of day
doctor visits	M	3	5	share these duties
discipline	M/Y	3	5	need more consistency
Read to	M/Y	2	5	more often – need regular time
Pick up after	M	3	4	wish you would help out
Play with	M/Y	3	5	NEED MORE TIME !!!
Talk with	M/Y	3	5	
Bathe	M	4	4	I like it
Put to bed	M/Y	3	4	work on resistance on her part
Respond at night	M	2	4	share this duty
Records/photos	Y	5	5	you are great about this

CONCERNS/PROBLEM AREAS

1. Guilt – am I spending enough time with my little girl?
2. No regular routine
3. Are you spending enough time with Avery?
4. Recent tantrums

GOALS—THIS YEAR

1. Develop regular, consistent routine
2. cut down on travel schedule
3. Each of us spend more & better time with Avery & as a family

GOALS—FUTURE

1. Healthy, loving, trusting child through our good parenting
2. no resentment on her part because we both worked full-time

PET PEEVES

Dropping Avery off at school - too traumatic !

CONCERNS ABOUT PARENTING AND MY PARTNERSHIP Do we agree on how to parent?
Afraid that tension is growing as a result of our not talking about and agreeing upon responsibilities and approaches. We need to set down some clear guidelines !

HEALTH
Physical Inventory, the exercise for this functional area, gives you the opportunity to grade yourselves on various components of your overall health and devise strategies, if necessary, for improving or maintaining it.

PHYSICAL INVENTORY

	A⁺	A	A⁻	B⁺	B	B⁻	C⁺	C	C⁻	D	F	GRADE NEXT YEAR	STRATEGY FOR MAKING THE GRADE
EATING HABITS/NUTRITION						✗						A⁻	more veggies "eat on run" less
EXERCISE										✗		B	more swimming
WEIGHT								✗				B⁺	↑
SLEEP							✗						better when baby sleeps all night/nap!
DENTAL			✗										
MEDICAL		✗											
ALCOHOL					✗							A⁻	drink less beer
STRESS			✗									A	need time away from baby / start work
DRUGS	✗												
EYES							✗					A⁻	get exam - need glasses?
GROOMING/ IMAGE								✗				B⁺	facial / lose weight talk to other new moms

LONG-TERM HEALTH GOALS	TIME FRAME
Get into great shape	before even thinking about another baby

TRAVEL

The exercise for this category is Leave of Absence. It gives you a chance to discuss and plan any trips or excursions for the coming year. It also asks you to describe your ideal vacation as a way to identify and compare priorities for vacation time.

LEAVE OF ABSENCE

TRIPS — EXCURSIONS — ADVENTURES

THIS YEAR		FUTURE	
WHERE	WHEN	WHERE	WHEN
Chicago	Thanksgiving	Paris	next year
San Francisco	spring	all the national	
Vancouver	summer	parks	?
DC	Dan's birthday	Scandinavia	within 5 years
		Rio	within 10 years

MY IDEAL VACATION

First week in a large city — sightseeing, visiting museums, galleries, viewing architecture, eating at fine restaurants and shopping.

Second week we take bikes and travel from inn to inn out in the country. Lots of photos, good food, wine tasting (ship some home)! Lots of exercise!

Our last week would be spent on the beach doing nothing but lying in the sun, eating fresh seafood, reading, and having lots of relaxed time for making love.

ENVIRONMENT

Environmental Effects asks you to identify important characteristics of your ideal environment—type of dwelling, neighborhood, community, geographic area—for various stages of your life so that you can begin making choices consistent with those objectives. It also gives you a chance to think about places you might like to experience sometime, enabling you to recognize and consider opportunities for relocation that may come your way.

ENVIRONMENTAL EFFECTS

TIME OF LIFE	TYPE OF DWELLING	NEIGHBORHOOD	COMMUNITY	GEOGRAPHIC AREA
present ↓ until we have kids	Apartment with lots of light for plants	Ethnic, lots of walk-to restaurants. close to a park/ public transportation	city-life activities	midwest or Eastern seaboard
young children	city townhouse with small garden	young families convenient to stores & park	"	same
10 years out	large house with land, lap pool. space for friends and family to stay	Family orientation "safe", friendly people	Good schools and services Political/Social awareness	New England
25 years out	same house for children (& grandchildren) plus a small Pied-à-terre in NYC!	Park or 5th Ave or Central Park West	NYC	NYC

PLACES I WOULD LIKE TO LIVE SOMETIME

WHERE	WHEN
Colorado ski town (for 1 season)	soon
Paris (1 year)	
Tropical Island (1 year)	

FRIENDS

The exercise for this area, The Company We Keep, asks you to list your friends and acquaintances in various categories. This can help you decide how to allocate your time and energy so as to keep high-priority friendships healthy.

THE COMPANY WE KEEP

BEST FRIENDS

MINE	OURS
Henry B.	Dave & Ann
Tazo	Andy & Clare
Roger	Martha
MaryAnn	Mario & Lucy
Chris	Carolyn
	Martins
	Stuart W.
	Paula

GOOD FRIENDS

MINE	OURS
Hugh	Holly
Lee Atkins	Diane
	BJ & Tina
	Betsy & Will
	Steins

CASUAL FRIENDS

MINE	OURS
Ginger Adams	Dave Brennan
Ward Bradley	John D'Angelo
Tom Slaby	Kroegers
	Duvalls

BUSINESS AND PROFESSIONAL FRIENDS

MINE	OURS
Marty Griggs	Thomases
Dick Hartley	Rob Thalken
Phil Jones	(and wife)
Trish	

PEOPLE TO GET TO KNOW BETTER

ME	US
Dan Bozeman	Clark & Cindy Hop
Dick & Karen Lehman	Mary & Greg
Gene S.	Jim & Dottie

THE SUMMIT MEETING

THE SUMMIT EXPERIENCE

Each Summit is a unique event shaped by the personalities, interests, attitudes, concerns, and objectives of the participants. Summits vary as much as the couples who undertake them. Because of the individual nature of the Summit experience, there is no way to predict exactly what yours will be like. However, this chapter conveys a sense of how those forty-eight hours might flow. It describes a representative Summit Meeting that proceeds according to the framework presented in the Summit Workbook. Imagine yourself there.

DAY ONE

All your planning and preparation is done and the big day has finally arrived. You arranged to leave work early to allow plenty of time for the drive to your Summit site. Somewhere along the way you stopped for a quiet dinner. When you arrive at the cabin you borrowed for your meeting (or hotel, or inn, or friend's home) you are excited, but a little nervous. After unpacking your bags, putting away the groceries, and taking out your completed Summit Exercises, you look at each other and say, "Well, what happens now?"

SUMMIT TALK—
GETTING STARTED

These first hours are critical to the success of your Summit because they set the tone for the remainder of the meeting. One of the first things to do after settling in is turn to The Summit Meeting section of the workbook. Here you will find a series of tasks called *Getting Started* that help ease the transition from daily life. Although the urge to plunge in and share your Summit Exercises may be great, restrain yourselves! *Getting Started* takes only about an hour and makes sharing your exercises even more worthwhile later on.

SUMMIT TIMETABLE

Completing the Summit Timetable, a detailed schedule of activities for your Summit Meeting, is the first task. Using the Summit Talk Agenda and Summit Logistics Planner from your Planning Meeting, you develop an hour-by-hour timetable that accounts for all your time until you depart for home.

When filling out the timetable, note that for the *Discussion and Decision-Making* phase of your Summit Talk you should probably allow at least one hour for each functional area. The functional areas can be discussed in any order that makes sense to you. If children are an overriding concern, it may be a good idea to discuss the functional area of Family before any others. If your jobs or career issues are a great concern, Work may be an appropriate first subject. You may choose to discuss all the functional areas in one day or take two days. The *Wrap-Up* phase requires one to two hours and should be scheduled for the end of your Summit Talk.

DEVELOPMENT OF SUMMIT TIMETABLE

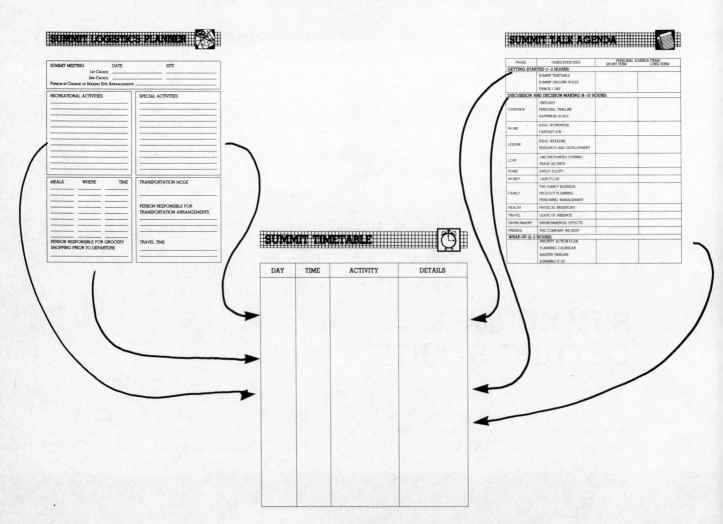

Of course, you will not follow your timetable exactly. As your Summit progresses you will find that some functional areas require more time than you initially scheduled, others less. You may decide to alter plans for recreational activities or meals, depending on the weather, your energy level, or how things are moving. Expect to make periodic adjustments to your timetable over the course of the forty-eight hours. Even with occasional fine tuning, the Summit Timetable serves as a reminder of the constraints on your time and gives you a way to manage it wisely. The example on page 92 illustrates how the hours of a Summit Meeting might be scheduled.

SUMMIT TIMETABLE

DAY	TIME	ACTIVITY	DETAILS
Friday	9:00	Summit Talk	Getting started Phase: Summit Timetable Summit Ground rules Things I like
Saturday	7:30	Breakfast	Here
	8:00	Summit Talk	Discussion & Decision Making Phase: Functional Areas: Work, Leisure, Money
	11:00	Recreation	Run
	12:00	Lunch	Here
	1:00	Summit Talk	Functional Areas: Home, Family, Health
	4:00	Recreation	Tennis, shower, nap.
	6:00	Summit Talk (over cocktails)	Functional Areas: Friends, Love
	8:00	Dinner Special Activity	Out Celebrate Anniversary
	9:30	Summit Talk (over dessert)	Functional Area: Environment
	10:30	Special Activity	Moonlight Stroll, Massage
Sunday	8:30	Recreation	Run, sauna
	9:30	Breakfast	Here
	10:30	Summit Talk	Functional Area: Travel
	11:15	Recreation	Hike
	12:30	Lunch	Picnic
	1:30	Summit Talk	Wrap-Up Phase: Priority Action Plan Planning Calendar Master Timeline Summing it up
	3:30	Recreation	Swim, sun
	5:00	Depart for home	

SUMMIT GROUND RULES

After completing your timetable, you move on to Summit Ground Rules, a task that gives you an opportunity to talk about how you are feeling at the outset of the Summit. Sharing these thoughts helps you relax and prepares you for the discussions that follow. You may find yourselves talking about talking, sharing ideas about what facilitates or inhibits your communication. Any guidelines that you agree will help you communicate more effectively during the Summit Talk are translated into Summit Ground Rules—parameters for action, behavior, or language that will prevail for the ensuing forty-eight hours.

No talking about that time in Mexico

No whining

No changing the subject until we both agree

No teasing

Breaks only when we both agree

THINGS I LIKE

Your final task in the *Getting Started* phase is to take a few minutes to write down ten things you like about your partner. Sharing supportive feelings with each other is a comforting way to confirm the basis for your relationship and your commitment to working things out, and sets a positive tone for your Summit.

THINGS I LIKE

THINGS I LIKE ABOUT

Jason

1. your hands

2. your blue eyes

3. your voice

4. your curiosity about the world

5. the way you laugh at my jokes

6. your ability to explain anything

7. your steamed vegetables

8. your patience

9. the way you kiss my neck

10. the way you put up with my messy room

THINGS I LIKE ABOUT

Marcia

1. your brains

2. your breasts

3. your ability to turn me on

4. your jokes

5. your family

6. your new bikini

7. your sense of humor

8. your organizational skills

9. your energy

10. your sensitivity to other people

The first hours of your Summit should leave you with a sense of anticipation and excitement about the upcoming discussions. After completing the introductory phase of the Summit Talk, you may decide to take a walk, go out for a nightcap, or jump into bed. You've gotten off to a good start, and when you wake up the next day you will begin the Summit in earnest, ready to talk and make some decisions about your life together.

DAY TWO

How you begin the first morning of your Summit Meeting is determined by the timetable you developed the night before. You may have scheduled a run, a game of tennis, a quiet walk, or perhaps breakfast in bed. Whatever you do should prepare you for the day's top priority: hours of intensive dialogue. When you are ready to start, gather pencils, paper, your Summit Exercises, and Discussion Guidelines, and settle into a comfortable place to talk.

SUMMIT TALK— DISCUSSION AND DECISION-MAKING

This phase of the Summit Talk is the greatest in duration and intensity. Discussions are guided by the Summit Talk Agenda, beginning with an overview and proceeding through each functional area. Although the time and energy you devote to individual functional areas will vary, the format for addressing each is the same:

1. Share your responses to the related Summit Exercise(s).
2. Use the Discussion Guidelines to discuss issues the exercises raised and reach agreement on areas of difference.
3. Discuss related personal agenda items.
4. Note plans, decisions, and commitments on the Action Plan.

SUMMIT EXERCISES

Sharing your Summit Exercises is the easiest way to begin the discussion of each functional area. You may want to take turns reading your own responses aloud, or exchange exercises and read each other's. It is up to you to select the format that is most comfortable and appropriate for the exercise you are reviewing. Your responses to the exercises will illuminate areas of simple disagreement and those of real conflict, dreams for the future, and personal expectations. As you share them, each new piece of information will help you understand yourself and your partner better.

COUPLE SHARING EXERCISES

DISCUSSION GUIDELINES

After sharing your Summit Exercise(s) for a particular functional area, talk about your reactions. The Discussion Guidelines provide ideas for addressing the issues raised by the exercises. They include questions that encourage you to resolve differences and make decisions and plans. During your discussions you may want to make notes about important points and ideas in the space provided on the Action Plan or on separate sheets of paper. You can refer to those notes when you fill in the Action Plan with final decisions and plans.

DISCUSSION GUIDELINES: WORK

HAPPINESS SCALE
- Why did you rate your level of satisfaction as you did?

IDEAL WORKWEEK
- What are the differences and similarities between your ideal workweek and a typical week now?

- How does your ideal week differ from your partner's? How is it similar?

- What does your description suggest about your interests and work style?

- What aspects of your current workweek (commute, location, people, duties) do you most enjoy? Least enjoy?

- Are there things you could do to make your current workweek more like your ideal? List those on the Action Plan.

FANTASY JOB

- Share and discuss your exercises.

- Are there surprises for either of you?

- What does your fantasy job say about your desires?

- Is there any chance your fantasy job might become a reality? How could you make it happen?

PERSONAL TIMELINE

- Talk about the career path you have outlined.

- How do your career aspirations mesh with your partner's?

- What factors are most influential in decisions (relocation, job change, time off) you make about your career?

- Do you anticipate a job or career change in the near or long-term future? If so, when? What will it be?

PERSONAL AGENDA ITEMS

Review your Summit Talk Agenda. Discuss any agenda items related to this functional area. List resolutions, actions, and plans on your Action Plan.

PERSONAL AGENDA ITEMS

On your Summit Talk Agenda you may have listed some personal items for the various functional areas. Make sure to address those after discussing each exercise. The following format might be helpful for talking about personal issues:

- Share thoughts, feelings, and ideas; discuss; negotiate
- Find a mutually satisfactory resolution
- Develop action plans.

ACTION PLANS

When you reach an agreement or make a decision, those resolutions should be recorded on the Action Plan for each functional area. The Action Plans are a way of keeping track of what happens at your Summit. They provide a record of the plans and strategies you devise. Putting your resolutions on paper ensures that you both understand what has been agreed to and have a similar set of expectations about your lives when you return home. The Action Plans are a blueprint from which you can work to implement your ideas. Action Plans specify:

what action is to be taken

who is responsible, and

date/time frame for completion.

ACTION PLAN: LEISURE

THINGS WE COULD DO TO MAKE THE WEEKEND MORE IDEAL:

spend at least one weekend night by ourselves
finish the deck so we can start using it
take turns planning a special date
go away no more than 2 weekends a month

ACTIVITIES/INTERESTS WE WILL PURSUE THIS YEAR:

NAME	ACTIVITY	HOW OFTEN/WHEN
Harry	lead Audubon	
	bird-watching tour	2 times
	start crew again	this spring
	submit reviews of	
	nature books	by Feb 1
Daphne	home quilt sales	2 times a yr.
	recipes on computer	by Jan 30
	yoga	once a week
	do story telling	
	at library	once a week

ACTIVITIES/INTERESTS WE WILL PURSUE TOGETHER THIS YEAR:

ACTIVITY	HOW OFTEN/WHEN
canoeing	4 times/summer, fall
folk dancing at the Y	spring session
volunteer for Greenpeace	during summer
organize walking tour of Charleston	Thanksgiving when family is here

NOTES: check on canoe rentals / find maps
send for Charleston info
learn to use computer
contact local Audubon society

COMMUNICATION TECHNIQUES FOR YOUR SUMMIT

Some of your Summit Talk will be highly personal, focusing on sensitive or emotionally weighty material. You may discover strong differences of opinion or encounter surprising and unexpected feelings that have never before been shared. Much of your talk will be fun, but some of it will be very trying. During the course of your conversations, you may get angry or impatient. And after hours of concentrated and intense discussion, you will be tired, perhaps frustrated. In order for your Summit to be successful, it is essential that communication is unobstructed and remains positive. While the structure of the Summit process supports communication, the quality of that communication is ultimately the responsibility of each couple. The following simple ideas and guidelines can help keep your discussions on a productive course. A bibliography at the end of this section offers other suggestions for readings that you may want to review before your Summit Meeting.

LISTENING

Listening is as important to communication as talking. Unfortunately, not many people have cultivated good listening skills. The problem can be especially acute for couples. People who live together can easily come to assume that they know what the other thinks and feels, so they tune each other out. Personal biases, fears, or insecurity can get in the way of a message that is being transmitted; partners filter it to fit their perceptions or needs, distorting the true meaning of what is being said. Often a person is too busy thinking about what he or she wants to say next to really listen to the point that is being made. All of these problems can disrupt communication. Employing some simple listening techniques during your Summit can improve the chances that you will hear and understand each other. When you listen:

- observe

- acknowledge

- encourage

- wait.

OBSERVATION is an important part of listening. Look for clues to the full message your partner is sending through body language. Pay attention to body position and eye contact. Listen not only to the words but also to the tone and volume of your partner's voice. Each of these is an important clue to the real message.

ACKNOWLEDGE what your partner is saying by occasionally paraphrasing what you hear, or ask for clarification. In this way you let your partner know you are really listening, as well as confirm that you understand what he or she is saying.

ENCOURAGE your partner with smiles, a nod of the head, or by looking into his or her eyes. Reassure him or her that you support the effort to speak honestly.

When all your attention is focused on your partner, he or she will be encouraged to continue.

WAIT for your partner to finish speaking before you voice your opinion. Hear your partner out. You will have plenty of time to express yourself. Allow your partner adequate time by not immediately rushing in with helpful advice or analysis.

TALKING

No matter how close couples are, talking about deep personal feelings or emotionally charged topics can be difficult. One major problem with male-female communication may be that men and women speak different languages. It has been suggested that some men perceive conversation as competition, so they tend to take control of a conversation in an attempt to "win." Their language focuses on things quantifiable, verifiable, and definite and is not conducive to expressing feelings or emotions. Women appear to view conversation more as an art form. Their language is more emotional, emphatic, and intense. It tends to be more deferential and cooperative.[13]

In order to overcome these inherent obstacles, partners must learn to decode and correctly interpret one another's language as well as create common terminology for important areas such as sex, housework, or money. Ingrained and habitual ways of speaking to one another are not suddenly going to disappear at the Summit. But the following suggestions can enhance your ability to engage in meaningful dialogue. When you talk:

- be prepared

- speak for yourself

- avoid control talk.

BE PREPARED. One of the best ways to facilitate good communication at your Summit is to arrive for the meeting fully prepared, knowing what it is you want to say. If you have spent time responding to the Summit Exercises, and have thoughtfully considered your personal agenda items, you should be well-versed in your own thoughts and feelings. Organizing your thoughts in your mind and on paper before you arrive at your Summit site will make it much easier to express them clearly and directly.

SPEAK FOR YOURSELF. Begin your statements with "I"—I think, I feel, I believe. Describe your own experience or reaction. Your partner cannot argue with the way you feel. Expressing your points in language that conveys your personal feelings is less threatening than accusing, attacking, or stating an absolute. Your partner is not going to leave you if he or she happens to disagree with what you say. Disagreement is inevitable between two individuals. Heated debate can be a healthy exercise for a couple if it ultimately leads to greater understanding and consensus.

AVOID CONTROL TALK. We all occasionally resort to control talk—efforts to control or manipulate conversation through techniques such as blaming, accusing, ridiculing, or criticizing.[14] In its passive forms, control talk is evidenced by complaining, whining, self-effacement, or changing the subject. Try to minimize these unproductive behaviors at your Summit. They will only frustrate your efforts to share and communicate.

NEGOTIATION

During the course of your talks, differences of opinion about how best to resolve an issue or about what constitutes an acceptable plan will undoubtedly arise. When that happens, you will have to negotiate a mutually acceptable solution. One negotiation technique, called *principled negotiation*, lends itself particularly well to the spirit of the Summit. In principled negotiation, participants are viewed as problem-solvers, not adversaries. The goal of the negotiation is a wise outcome, reached efficiently and amicably.[15] This method of negotiation makes great sense for the Summit. The following discussion of some of the important aspects of principled negotiation relies heavily on the theories Roger Fisher and William Ury outlined in their book *Getting to Yes*. When you negotiate:

- separate the people from the problem

- focus on interests, not positions

- invent options for mutual gain

- use objective criteria.

SEPARATE THE PEOPLE FROM THE PROBLEM as you attempt to settle differences. A couple has two interests in their negotiation. One is solving the problem, the other is maintaining their relationship. While emotions may play a large role in negotiations, try to distinguish between the way you feel about a particular problem and how you feel about your partner. Express and interpret comments as problem identification rather than personal attack.

FOCUS ON INTERESTS, NOT POSITIONS as you work through conflict. Don't get hung up on a hard-line position that prevents you from discovering a workable solution. Remain flexible to achieve your desired goals.

INVENT OPTIONS FOR MUTUAL GAIN by thinking creatively about alternatives. Try to come up with a number of possible solutions (no matter how unlikely they seem) from which the final solution can be shaped. Brainstorming is most successful when participants are not afraid of being criticized for their ideas. Develop as many ideas as you can before you start to evaluate them. If you can identify shared interests (such as saving time, getting exercise, or seeing friends) you will be better able to find solutions that satisfy you both. When interests differ, explore ways to accommodate both partners' desires. Remember, you are having a Summit to work things out *together*.

USE OBJECTIVE CRITERIA to judge the merit of a final decision. This is not as easy in a negotiation between personal partners as it might be between a car salesman and prospective buyer, or employee and supervisor. Standards such as market value, cost, precedent, and efficiency are not always feasible for personal areas such as sex, money, housework, and child care. It is hard to assign a value to such things as keeping in touch with friends or sending birthday cards, even though you might agree that these things are worthwhile. Partners must develop a personal set of standards and criteria for evaluating decisions based on the goals and priorities they have identified for their relationship. Once you have established the criteria for decision-making (and there may be more than one standard), present your solutions in terms of those standards. Keep in mind you must reason and be open to reason if you are to resolve your differences satisfactorily.

TIME-OUT FROM SUMMIT TALK

RECREATION

After talking for several hours, you will be more than ready for a break. The intense dialogue of the Summit can be exhilarating, but also exhausting. Your mind, as well as your body, will benefit from occasional time-outs. Exercise your body, relax your mind, and take a few moments for yourself during the hour or two in the middle of the day that you've scheduled for recreation. You will return to your talks feeling energized and ready to plunge in again. Even an occasional five-minute stretch will help you remain alert and attentive during your discussions.

SPECIAL ACTIVITIES

The second evening of your Summit should be very special. It may be the first time in a long while that the two of you have had the chance to enjoy each other without distraction. Despite the emotional ups and downs of the day, you will feel closer to your partner. The special activities you plan, which may range from dancing to the radio to recalling every detail of your first date, will enhance that closeness. However you decide to celebrate, this part of your Summit will make you feel good about being together.

MEALS

You may decide to discuss some of the functional areas over breakfast, lunch, or dinner. Topics such as Travel, Leisure, or Friends lend themselves to discussion over cocktails, a meal, or dessert. Or you may use mealtime as a well-deserved rest, a complete break from your Summit Talk. You might take some of the time allocated for meals to be alone and reflect, to prepare for the next functional area, or just go out for some fresh air. As emphasized earlier, you can always make adjustments in the timetable as your Summit progresses.

By the end of the first full day of your Summit you will feel drained. But you should also feel confident that your diligence and effort will pay off as your partnership begins to take on the positive characteristics of a well-managed enterprise.

DAY THREE

SUMMIT TALK—WRAP-UP

The final day and phase of your Summit is devoted to summarizing plans, working out details, and bringing your Summit Meeting to a satisfactory conclusion. Over the course of the previous two days you will have talked about a wide variety of subjects. If the decisions and plans you made are to be successfully implemented, you must reach final agreement and develop final plans for action at home.

PRIORITY ACTION PLAN

The Priority Action Plan is an account of the major activities or tasks that you are committed to fulfilling, individually and together, in the coming year. Posting the Priority Action Plan in a conspicuous place when you get home will make it much more likely that you follow through with those commitments.

PRIORITY ACTION PLAN

NAME		NAME	
Mike		*Heidi*	
ACTION	TARGET DATE/ TIME FRAME	ACTION	TARGET DATE/ TIME FRAME
Plumbing repairs	by 2/5	start collecting info on African safaris	next month
buy summer concert series tickets	by 3/1	fund / decide on pre-school for Carla	by 3/15
pay bills / correspondence	regular time: Monday nights	hire gardener	by 2/15
lose 10 lbs	by 4/15	plan dinner with Browns	before they leave
Plan "Enchanted Evening"	to take place this summer	talk to Janet about transfer to new division	by 1/30
Go to city	once a month		→
Pick wallpaper for Dining room	by 2/5		→
		implement new division of responsibility (see home action plan)	
enroll in wine class	by 1/15	sign up for wind surfing lessons	this summer

PLANNING CALENDAR

The Planning Calendar provides an overview of the coming twelve months. On it you highlight major events, trips, and important plans on a monthly basis as a reminder of arrangements to be made, time to be taken off, or schedules to be rearranged. It is not a detailed day-by-day calendar, but rather the year at a glance.

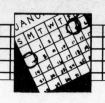

MONTH: February

Pop visits for
a week

Valentine's Ball

MONTH: March

Mom & Dad's 30th
wedding anniversary
celebration

MONTH: April

Start tennis group
MEXICO ☼

Associates meeting

MONTH: May

Celebrate 2nd
Anniversary—
Sailing weekend

MONTH: June

Begin house
renovation

Aaron's graduation
Rafting trip

MONTH: July

Keep open to
manage renovation

Barb & Abby visit
(where will they stay?)

MONTH: August

Backpack weekend
with Hobbs

Tennis tournament
with Andi & Jeff

MONTH: September

Conference—
Las Vegas

MONTH: October

Rachel's class
reunion

Give Halloween
party

MONTH: November

Thanksgiving
with Aunt Eve

Yosemite with
Linda & Clay

MONTH: December

Holidays in Vail

MONTH: January

Next Summit

MASTER TIMELINE

The Master Timeline is a joint outline for your life, highlighting important events, transitions, and plans that you both would like to see as part of your future. It provides a map for your partnership that, as time passes, will be refined and modified.

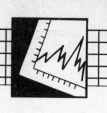

YEAR OR AGE	Now	1988	1990	1992	1996	2010	2015
WORK	reign worker 1/2 - 3/4 time →					Birth Nature (ha-ha)	
LEISURE	Prioritise golf midnight sailing						
LOVE	always celebrate Anniversary away, alone together						
HOME		Buy Hobbo					
MONEY				Set up trusts when kids are born			
FAMILY		1st child	2nd child	3rd child			
HEALTH	always stay in shape (home gym?)						
TRAVEL	Israel Greece					25th Anniversary in Bali	
ENVIRON-MENT	City	'Burbs				Great Lakes Family Vacation Home	
FRIENDS	Always important				Travel occasionally with good friends		

SUMMING IT UP

This is the final task of the *Wrap-Up* phase and of the Summit. It gives you a chance to reflect on your Summit experience, summarize what you have learned, and highlight your priorities.

KEY WORDS TO DESCRIBE OUR LIFE IN THE COMING YEAR:

Vitality
Sponteneity   Fun
         Friends   Togetherness

KEY VALUES THAT WILL GUIDE OUR LIVES:

commitment to our relationship
giving something back to society
keeping friendships alive and healthy

WORDS THAT DESCRIBE OUR SUMMIT:

intense, difficult, rewarding, humorous (at times!)
special.

THE MOST IMPORTANT THINGS WE LEARNED ABOUT OURSELVES:

NAME: carol

how much I like working
apprehension about career/
     motherhood balance

NAME: John

how much I dislike my job
how much I want to get
     into politics

THE MOST IMPORTANT THINGS WE LEARNED ABOUT EACH OTHER:

NAME: carol

How much your "identity"
is tied up in your job

NAME: John

how important your family
traditions are to you
how important it is for me to
give you credit for your work

THE MOST IMPORTANT THINGS WE LEARNED ABOUT OUR RELATIONSHIP:

how much we love each other
how hard it is for us to talk about sex.
how important it is for each of us to have our own friends
need to work out conflict over having children

DATE FOR FOLLOW-UP MEETING:

January 20

WE NEED MORE TIME!

If you finish early on the third day, you might decide to spend the rest of the time relaxing and enjoying your Summit site. However, it is very possible that there just won't be enough time to address all the items on your agenda. One exercise may lead you off on a discussion of tangential issues, taking away from the time you had scheduled for other functional areas. You may find that an ostensibly simple issue masks a complex set of problems. Falling behind can happen for a variety of reasons. If you sense you are running out of time, don't succumb to the desire to rush through important topics. Instead, postpone discussion until you both have more time and energy.

If, as you near the end of the forty-eight hours, you realize you will not be able to cover all the items on your agenda, you should:

1. Reach closure on the subjects that you have addressed and make sure that any Action Plans related to those areas are completed.
2. Decide when and where to finish your Summit—try to estimate how long it will take, schedule a time and place to do it—and add it to your Priority Action Plan.

You may find you are unable to reach agreement on certain decisions or come to a mutually satisfactory resolution to particular problems. If that occurs:

1. Decide what must happen before you can reach an agreement— perhaps you need more information or the issue deserves more contemplation.
2. Choose a time when you will attempt to resolve the outstanding issues—later in your Summit or sometime after you return home.
3. Devise an action plan for unresolved issues that includes responsibilities and the time or date when you will deal with them again.

It is important not to leave any issues unresolved; otherwise they will continue to be a source of irritation after you get home. Force yourselves to come to a conclusion even if it's merely deciding when to address a subject again.

MEETING ADJOURNED

By the conclusion of your personal Summit you will know much more about yourself and your relationship and should feel stronger and more in control of your partnership. You will have established goals and devised strategies to attain them. You will have a better sense of your respective roles. You will have participated in a process of shared decision-making, increasing the chances that those plans will work. You will have learned a lot about communication—what works and what doesn't. And you will have spent some time nurturing your relationship in ways that are not always possible at home. Life is not suddenly going to be perfect after your first Summit. But you will have taken a big step forward.

CHERYL: "Each Summit we have is unpredictable, but also familiar because we use the parts that work well over and over again. Like a timetable, for example. It wasn't until we were in the midst of our first Summit that we realized how quickly forty-eight hours could pass. Without a timetable, it took us a long time to decide when to take breaks, what to do about meals, and in what order to discuss our agenda items. That time was taken away from the hours we had to devote to the real purpose of the Summit. Using a timetable, like the one in the Summit Workbook, has made subsequent Summits much more productive. Another part of the Summit that never changes is my excitement about reading Charley's Summit Exercises. I know how hard it is for him to find the time to do the exercises, which makes everything I learn from them more meaningful. After sharing our exercises, we look forward to the second evening of our Summit—it is a special night for us. We're happy to have made it through an entire day of talking and plan the evening as a complete break. Usually we go for a cross-country ski (our Summits are always in January). We have a good bottle of wine with dinner and splurge on a great dessert. Since we are also away from our daughter, we end the evening with a quiet walk together, a favorite activity from pre-parent days. This evening doesn't vary much from Summit to Summit. It represents the pinnacle of the experience to us, before starting the long trip to the next Summit. The last morning we really begin to make progress on our plans. We would never follow through with them if we didn't have a list and a calendar to post when we got home. I usually compile the Priority Action Plan while Charley reads through the notes we have diligently taken. It isn't tedious—the Wrap-Up phase is a chance for us to review what we've talked about, finalize decisions, and reflect on our Summit. Wrapping things up before we leave gears us up for the hectic scene that awaits our return. At home, the stack of Summit folders we are accumulating represents a huge investment of our time and effort. But even more, they represent our dedication to managing our life together, making it as full of fun, challenge, adventure, and opportunity as we can. The Summit is the only way we can do that."

LISA: By the end of a Summit weekend, we feel as if we've been through the wringer emotionally, mentally, and physically. But we wouldn't trade that feeling for anything. Most of the excitement is generated by sharing our responses to the exercises. Inevitably, one of us comes up with some answers that shock and surprise. But we are equally likely to discover that we hold exactly the same attitude or outlook about a particular issue. Some discussions can be really boring—for instance, trying to establish financial priorities. In those cases we reward ourselves with a break if we make it through. Fortunately, Boegy is a diligent scribe so we always have a detailed summary of what goes on during our Summit—even those things I would prefer to forget. We've learned a lot about communicating as a result of our talks. For instance, Boegy speaks more slowly and tentatively than I do about emotional matters. I finally understood that if I wanted him to express himself, I would have to give him the time to do so and not try to speak for him. We've made it a tradition to repeat our wedding vows on the second night of each Summit. It's kind of corny, but no matter how difficult life has been in the past twelve months, reaffirming our commitment gives us a measure of strength for the coming year. When we finally finish with the last item on our agenda, we are overcome with a sense of relief, but also some sadness that our Summit is over. Few experiences make us feel as close and connected as this one."

CHAPTER 8

MANAGING YOUR LIFE TOGETHER

The Summit process doesn't end when partners return home from their two-day retreat. In fact, this is where it begins in earnest. Once home, the challenge remains of putting all the ideas generated at the Summit into action. Unfortunately, plans that seemed so reasonable when they were devised in a mountain cabin can feel painfully unfeasible when a couple opens the door to a dirty house, a stack of unpaid bills, and a phone message to fly to Detroit the next day.

Providing a detailed framework for this part of the Summit process is not possible. From here on, partners must forge their own way. Remember, things are not going to change overnight. Success in this stage demands hard work, persistence, and patience. The following ideas have helped us manage our lives between Summits.

GETTING DOWN TO BUSINESS

The first thing to do after returning home is post the Priority Action Plan, and any other Action Plans, in a prominent place where you will see them every day. The Action Plans will remind you of the commitments made at your Summit. As you complete a task or follow through with a plan, cross it off your list and congratulate yourself. The Planning Calendar should also be posted in a central location. It serves as the rough schedule of events for the year ahead and will remind you of the priorities established for each month. Finally, file your Summit Exercises and the notes you took during your Summit discussions in a folder or three-ring binder with the date of your Summit. If you decide to make the Summit Meeting an annual event, the notes from previous Summits provide an interesting, nostalgic, and humorous basis for comparison.

THE FOLLOW-UP MEETING

Two or three weeks after the Summit Meeting partners should meet for a couple of hours to evaluate the experience and assess their progress in implementing plans. The Follow-Up Exercise should be filled out by each partner and brought to the meeting as a basis for discussion. You will probably discover that you have accomplished a great deal since the Summit. However, you may decide that certain goals were unrealistic or, because of new information, some plans must be changed. The Follow-up Meeting is the time to reevaluate and revise plans.

minder about, such as ticket order forms, schedules, or invitations. How often have you clipped an advertisement for a concert from the newspaper and filed it in a stack on your desk or bureau only to find it the day after the concert or when all tickets have been sold? By putting all social, recreational, and cultural activity reminders in one place you can continually review them, decide what you want to do, and successfully follow up on those plans. On our bulletin boards you might find:

- A Stanford football season ticket order form
- An invitation to a political fund-raiser
- A coupon for a free pitcher of beer at a local pub
- The schedule of movies for the local one-night-run movie theater
- An invitation to a cocktail party
- A schedule of baby gym classes.

MESSAGE BOARD

A chalkboard, drymark board, or designated area to post notes is a great way to exchange bits of information. You can use these boards to:

- Give each other reminders: "See you at Chez Panisse tonight at 8:00," or "Put any dry cleaning in the hall so I can take it with me tomorrow."
- Say nice things to each other: "Last night was great," or "Thanks for picking up my shirts."
- Ask questions: "What was the amount of the check you wrote to Eddie Bauer? I can't balance the checkbook!" or "Would you mind picking up the wine for the party?"

We date these notes so there will be fewer misunderstandings. Of course, all of these things could be said out loud. But with busy schedules it is easy to forget to ask or tell our partners something important.

IN-BOX

The last essential communication tool in our homes is an in-box. The in-box functions as the designated place to put documents, letters, checks that need signing, papers that need filing, articles that we want our partner to see.

You probably have some kind of communication system operating in your home now. Simple tactics like those described above can improve the flow of mundane information, so that when you have time together you can talk about interesting things instead of haranguing because nobody arranged for a baby-sitter or arguing because your partner forgot to tell you about the business dinner to which you were both invited. Organizing the flow of information helps improve communication.

PARTNERS' MEETING

Another essential part of managing our lives is a regular partners' meeting. One night a week is set aside to be alone with our partner, just to talk. We don't accept invitations for social engagements or make plans with friends on that night. Usually we have dinner in a quiet restaurant. We prepare a short agenda of things we want to discuss, and over dinner and wine we talk about decisions that have to be made, plans that must be confirmed, or anything that has been bothering us. We catch up on the news of our lives. We compare calendars for the upcoming weeks. When all our "business" has been taken care of, we enjoy being with each other. We have made this time together a top priority in a busy week.

A partners' meeting does not have to be dinner out. It may be a get-together in bed over a cup of hot chocolate on Wednesday nights. It may be a regular Sunday morning brunch or a Saturday afternoon walk. The important thing is to set aside a certain amount of time for the two of you that you dedicate to talking about what is on your mind and sharing the important information in your lives. This is not easy to do, particularly if you have children. But once you make it a tradition, you'll find it an indispensable part of your week.

ROMANCE

Part of managing our lives is making special time for ourselves. While we all enjoy spontaneity in love, it doesn't hurt to also plan ways to keep the romance alive. We try to go away at least once every six or eight weeks even if it's only for one night at a motel in the next town. In the interim, we try to use some forethought to nurture the passion in our daily lives. Little things, like bringing home a bottle of champagne, planning a surprise sunset picnic, or tucking a love note into your partner's briefcase, are as important as the other managerial tasks for keeping your partnership healthy.

MAKING THE SUMMIT AN ANNUAL EVENT

We view the Summit as an ongoing process, not a once-in-a-lifetime experience. We have attempted to incorporate the spirit of the Summit—a commitment to communication, sharing, and planning—into our daily lives. Each year we plan a two-day Summit Meeting to assess the past year and look forward to the coming twelve months. We, and other friends, schedule our Summit Meetings for the same time each year so that it becomes a regular check-in point. Some people like to tie their annual Summits to a special event, such as an anniversary. Others have found that January is an ideal time because the whole year lies ahead. The knowledge that we have an annual Summit gives us a great sense of security as well as a feeling of order and control. It helps us manage on a daily basis.

The focus of each Summit changes as our lives change. Our agenda reflects the issues that are important at the time. Some Summit Meetings are better than others. A few have seemed like complete failures; others have been magnificent successes. Each Summit has, however, offered something of value. We always come away with a deeper understanding of ourselves, each other, and our relationship.

THE MINI-SUMMIT

If, during the year between annual Summit Meetings, we feel that a particular issue needs attention, a special problem needs solving, or a pressing decision needs to be made, we schedule a Mini-Summit. Sometimes we hold a Mini-Summit to follow up on an issue that was not fully resolved at the Summit Meeting. The Mini-Summit resembles the Summit Meeting in many respects. It takes place away from home. Discussion, whether limited to one or a variety of topics, revolves around a predetermined agenda. It follows a format of discussion, negotiation, and decision-making, with or without the help of exercises. A Mini-Summit does not have to extend over two days. It might be a six-hour meeting focused on the single issue of career changes. Or it might be a twenty-four-hour retreat to review several functional areas.

SUMMING IT UP

The Summit process has helped us integrate lessons from management into our partnerships by providing the framework for setting goals, exploring roles, and making decisions together. It has helped us hone our communication skills while continually reinforcing our belief that ongoing, effective communication is the critical element for maintaining a good relationship. It has given us the opportunity to spend time with our partners in a way that nourishes and strengthens our love.

The Summit process demands determination, stamina, creativity, and patience. It involves risk, but we think it's worth it. In this changing world, partners who do not take responsibility for their own happiness and the success of their partnership stand little chance of working things out. With the help of the Summit process, you can begin bettering your chances.

NOTES

1. Victor Fuchs, *How We Live* (Cambridge, Mass.: Harvard University Press, 1983), p. 147.
2. Philip Blumstein and Pepper Schwartz, *American Couples* (New York: William Morrow, 1983), p. 45.
3. Wenda Brewster O'Reilly (doctoral dissertation), "Where Equal Opportunity Fails: Corporate Men and Women in Dual Career Families," Stanford University, Stanford, CA.
4. Blumstein and Schwartz, p. 77.
5. Ibid, p. 76.
6. Ibid, p. 65.
7. Ibid, p. 145.
8. Letty Cottin Pogrebin, *Family Politics* (New York: McGraw-Hill, 1983), p. 145.
9. Blumstein and Schwartz, p. 146.
10. Fuchs, p. 147.
11. Thomas Peters and Robert Waterman, *In Search of Excellence: Lessons from America's Best-Run Companies* (New York: Harper & Row, 1982), Chapter 8.
12. Philip Shenon, "Getting Ahead—and Staying Married," *The New York Times*, March 6, 1983.
13. Steven Naifeh and Gregory White Smith, *Why Can't Men Open Up? Overcoming Men's Fear of Intimacy* (New York: Clarkson N. Potter, Inc., 1984), pp. 69–70.
14. Sherod Miller, Ph.D., Daniel Wackman, Ph.D., et al., *Straight Talk: A New Way to Get Closer to Others by Saying What You Really Mean* (New York: New American Library, 1982), pp. 29–30.
15. Roger Fisher and William Ury, *Getting to Yes: Negotiating Agreement Without Giving In* (New York: Penguin Books, 1983).

BIBLIOGRAPHY

Blanchard, Kenneth, and Spencer Johnson. *The One-Minute Manager*. New York: William Morrow, 1982.

Blumstein, Philip, and Pepper Schwartz. *American Couples*. New York: William Morrow, 1983.

Bolles, Richard N. *What Color Is Your Parachute?* Berkeley, Calif.: Ten Speed Press, 1977.

Dowling, Colette. *The Cinderella Complex*. New York: Summit Books, 1981.

Fisher, Roger, and William Ury. *Getting to Yes: Negotiating Agreement Without Giving In*. New York: Penguin Books, 1981.

Friedan, Betty. *The Second Stage*. New York: Summit Books, 1981.

Gilligan, Carol. *In a Different Voice: Psychological Theory and Women's Development*. Cambridge: Harvard University Press, 1982.

Hall, Francine, and Douglas Hall. *The Two-Career Couple*. Reading, Pa.: Addison-Wesley Publishing Co., 1979.

Levinson, Daniel J., et al. *The Seasons of a Man's Life*. New York: Alfred A. Knopf, 1978.

Naifeh, Steven, and Gregory White Smith. *Why Can't Men Open Up? Overcoming Men's Fear of Intimacy*. New York: Clarkson N. Potter, Inc., 1984.

Peters, Thomas, and Robert Waterman, Jr. *In Search of Excellence: Lessons from America's Best-Run Companies*. New York: Harper & Row, 1982.

Pogrebin, Letty Cottin. *Family Politics*. New York: McGraw-Hill, 1983.

———. *Growing Up Free*. New York: McGraw-Hill, 1980.

Shaevitz, Marjorie Hansen. *The Superwoman Syndrome*. New York: Warner Books, 1984.

Shaevitz, Marjorie Hansen, and Morton H. Shaevitz. *Making It Together as a Two-Career Couple*. Boston: Houghton Mifflin, 1980.

PART THREE

THE
SUMMIT
WORKBOOK

HOW TO USE THE SUMMIT WORKBOOK

The Summit Workbook is designed to guide you through your first Summit by providing material that will facilitate the process. For ease and convenience, all the pages in the workbook are detachable. The workbook is divided into four sections corresponding to the four stages of the Summit process.

SECTION ONE:
THE PLANNING MEETING

This section includes the tasks you must complete at your Planning Meeting: Summit Contract, Summit Logistics Planner, Summit Agenda Planner, and Summit Talk Agenda. You may wish to refer back to Chapter 5 for a detailed description of this stage. Once you have finished these tasks, make the necessary arrangements for baby-sitters, time off from work, travel, or whatever is necessary prior to your departure. Most important: Set up enough time before leaving to complete your Summit Exercises.

SECTION TWO:
THE SUMMIT EXERCISES

In this section are the Summit Exercises and instructions. There are two copies of each exercise so that you and your partner can work independently. If you have any questions about how to fill out the exercises, Chapter 6 provides a complete description and example of each.

SECTION THREE:
THE SUMMIT MEETING

This section contains the materials you will need at your Summit Meeting. These include a series of *Getting Started* tasks—Summit Timetable, Summit Ground Rules, and Things I Like. It also provides Discussion Guidelines for talking about your exercises, and Action Plans on which to note the decisions and plans you make for each functional area. Finally, this section includes a series of *Wrap-Up* tasks—Priority Action Plan, Planning Calendar, Master Timeline, and Summing It Up—that are meant to help you organize and articulate all you have accomplished during your Summit. Refer to Chapter 7 for a detailed description of the Summit Meeting.

SECTION FOUR:
MANAGING YOUR LIFE TOGETHER

The final section contains the tasks to be completed after your Summit Meeting. A few weeks after you return home, you should turn to this section. At a short Follow-Up Meeting, you can discuss your responses to the Follow-Up Exercise and make any revisions on the Follow-Up Action Plan. Review Chapter 8 for ideas and suggestions about integrating the Summit process into your daily lives.

If you are ready to proceed with your Summit, set a date for your Planning Meeting. At your Planning Meeting, simply turn to the next page and begin the tasks. You will be on your way to the Summit!

THE PLANNING MEETING

SUMMIT CONTRACT

RESOLVED:

We are committed to engage in the Summit process as partners. We will take the time to plan our Summit Meeting and complete the Summit Exercises. We will reserve 48 consecutive hours for our Summit. Together we will share, explore, discuss, and resolve issues of concern. We will strive to maintain open and honest communication in an atmosphere of respect and trust. We will utilize our inner resources as individuals and our unique strength as a couple to improve communication, make mutually acceptable decisions, and plan for our future.

AMENDMENTS:

_____

_____

_____

_____

_____

_____

_____

_____

_____

_____ _____

_____

_____

SIGNED: _____ SIGNED: _____

DATE: _____ DATE: _____

SUMMIT CONTRACT

Read the contract carefully. Modify or amend it in any way to reflect your interests and intentions. Then sign it to signify your commitment to the Summit process.

SUMMIT LOGISTICS PLANNER

SUMMIT MEETING   DATE   SITE
                1st Choice _____ _____
                2nd Choice _____ _____
Person in Charge of Making Site Arrangements _____

RECREATIONAL ACTIVITIES

_____
_____
_____
_____
_____
_____
_____
_____
_____
_____
_____
_____
_____
_____

SPECIAL ACTIVITIES

_____
_____
_____
_____
_____
_____
_____
_____
_____
_____
_____
_____
_____

MEALS   WHERE   TIME

_____ _____ _____
_____ _____ _____
_____ _____ _____
_____ _____ _____
_____ _____ _____
_____ _____ _____
_____ _____ _____

PERSON RESPONSIBLE FOR GROCERY
SHOPPING PRIOR TO DEPARTURE

_____
_____

TRANSPORTATION MODE

_____

PERSON RESPONSIBLE FOR
TRANSPORTATION ARRANGEMENTS

_____
_____
_____

TRAVEL TIME

_____
_____

SUMMIT LOGISTICS PLANNER

Choose a date and select a site for your Summit. Decide who will make site arrangements.

Decide what recreational and special activities you want to include at your Summit.

Determine how you will handle meals and who is responsible for grocery shopping.

Settle transportation details.

SUMMIT AGENDA PLANNER

FUNCTIONAL AREA	PERSONAL AGENDA ITEMS	
	SHORT-TERM	LONG-TERM
WORK		
LEISURE		
LOVE		
HOME		
MONEY		
FAMILY		
HEALTH		
TRAVEL		
ENVIRONMENT		
FRIENDS		

SUMMIT AGENDA PLANNER

Together, brainstorm about all the topics you want to discuss at your Summit. On the Summit Agenda Planner, list each topic under the appropriate functional area, distinguishing between short- and long-term issues.

SUMMIT TALK AGENDA

PHASE	TASKS/EXERCISES	PERSONAL AGENDA ITEMS	
		SHORT-TERM	LONG-TERM
GETTING STARTED (1–2 HOURS)			
	SUMMIT TIMETABLE		
	SUMMIT GROUND RULES		
	THINGS I LIKE		
DISCUSSION AND DECISION-MAKING (8–10 HOURS)			
OVERVIEW	OBITUARY		
	PERSONAL TIMELINE		
	HAPPINESS SCALE		
WORK	IDEAL WORKWEEK		
	FANTASY JOB		
LEISURE	IDEAL WEEKEND		
	RESEARCH AND DEVELOPMENT		
LOVE	ONE ENCHANTED EVENING		
	TRADE SECRETS		
HOME	SWEAT EQUITY		
MONEY	CASH FLOW		
FAMILY	THE FAMILY BUSINESS		
	PRODUCT PLANNING		
	PERSONNEL MANAGEMENT		
HEALTH	PHYSICAL INVENTORY		
TRAVEL	LEAVE OF ABSENCE		
ENVIRONMENT	ENVIRONMENTAL EFFECTS		
FRIENDS	THE COMPANY WE KEEP		
WRAP-UP (2–3 HOURS)			
	PRIORITY ACTION PLAN		
	PLANNING CALENDAR		
	MASTER TIMELINE		
	SUMMING IT UP		

SUMMIT TALK AGENDA

Transfer all items you agree you would like to discuss at your Summit from the Summit Agenda Planner to the appropriate section of the Summit Talk Agenda. This agenda will provide the outline for discussion at your Summit Meeting.

THE SUMMIT
EXERCISES

OBITUARY

OBITUARY

Assume you are looking back over your life and write your obituary as you would like to be remembered. Describe personal and professional achievements, family, public service, where you lived, and any other important personal history. Include at what age, how, and where you died.

OBITUARY

OBITUARY

Assume you are looking back over your life and write your obituary as you would like to be remembered. Describe personal and professional achievements, family, public service, where you lived, and any other important personal history. Include at what age, how, and where you died.

YEAR OR AGE	WORK	LEISURE	LOVE	HOME	MONEY	FAMILY	HEALTH	TRAVEL	ENVIRON-MENT	FRIENDS

PERSONAL TIMELINE

Number the top axis of your timeline in yearly increments that make sense for you. Now, imagine your life unfolding exactly as you would wish. Fill in the timeline to reflect this ideal vision noting milestones, important events, and relevant details in each functional area. The following questions may stimulate your thinking.

Work	What kind? Where?
Leisure	How would free time be spent?
Love	Romantic highpoints?
Home	What kind? How many? Where?
Money	Income level at various times? From what sources?
Family	Children? How many? When? Extended family relations?
Health	How would you keep mind, body, and soul in shape?
Travel	Where? When? With whom?
Environment	Preferred locations for living, working, playing?
Friends	Who? How important?

YEAR OR AGE	WORK	LEISURE	LOVE	HOME	MONEY	FAMILY	HEALTH	TRAVEL	ENVIRON-MENT	FRIENDS

PERSONAL TIMELINE

Number the top axis of your timeline in yearly increments that make sense for you. Now, imagine your life unfolding exactly as you would wish. Fill in the timeline to reflect this ideal vision noting milestones, important events, and relevant details in each functional area. The following questions may stimulate your thinking.

Work	What kind? Where?
Leisure	How would free time be spent?
Love	Romantic highpoints?
Home	What kind? How many? Where?
Money	Income level at various times? From what sources?
Family	Children? How many? When? Extended family relations?
Health	How would you keep mind, body, and soul in shape?
Travel	Where? When? With whom?
Environment	Preferred locations for living, working, playing?
Friends	Who? How important?

	WORK	LEISURE	LOVE	HOME	MONEY	HEALTH	TRAVEL	ENVIRONMENT	FRIENDS	FAMILY
10										
9										
8										
7										
6										
5										
4										
3										
2										
1										

HAPPINESS SCALE

Complete the scale by drawing a horizontal line across each bar at the number that best represents your current level of satisfaction in each functional area. Also, rate your overall level of happiness.

Happiness Scale: 10 = Totally satisfied; 1 = Absolutely miserable.

HAPPINESS SCALE

10										
9										
8										
7										
6										
5										
4										
3										
2										
1										
	WORK	LEISURE	LOVE	HOME	MONEY	HEALTH	TRAVEL	ENVIRONMENT	FRIENDS	FAMILY

HAPPINESS SCALE

Complete the scale by drawing a horizontal line across each bar at the number that best represents your current level of satisfaction in each functional area. Also, rate your overall level of happiness.

Happiness Scale: 10 = Totally satisfied; 1 = Absolutely miserable.

IDEAL WORKWEEK

TIME	MONDAY	TUESDAY	WEDNESDAY	THURSDAY	FRIDAY
M O R N I N G					
A F T E R N O O N					
E V E N I N G					

IDEAL WORKWEEK

Imagine waking up next Monday morning with the opportunity to experience the perfect workweek. Complete this exercise by indicating how you would ideally spend those five days.

Would you work at your current job or another?

Would you work every day? For how many hours?

How much time would you spend with family? Friends? Your partner?

What other activities would engage you?

IDEAL WORKWEEK

TIME	MONDAY	TUESDAY	WEDNESDAY	THURSDAY	FRIDAY
M O R N I N G					
A F T E R N O O N					
E V E N I N G					

IDEAL WORKWEEK

Imagine waking up next Monday morning with the opportunity to experience the perfect workweek. Complete this exercise by indicating how you would ideally spend those five days.

Would you work at your current job or another?

Would you work every day? For how many hours?

How much time would you spend with family? Friends? Your partner?

What other activities would engage you?

FANTASY JOB

POSITION: _____

RESPONSIBILITIES/DUTIES: _____
_____
_____
_____
_____
_____

AGE: _____

LOCATION: _____

HIGHLIGHTS/ACCOMPLISHMENTS: _____
_____
_____
_____
_____
_____
_____

NOTES: _____
_____
_____

FANTASY JOB

Imagine that you are given the opportunity, for one year, to hold any job or position you desire. You could be the president of the country, a research scientist, a ballet dancer, a sports writer, or a wilderness guide—anything you want. During this period you would not have to worry about finances or how the job would affect your personal or professional life.

What job or position would you choose?

What age would you be?

What would you hope to accomplish, learn, or do in that year?

FANTASY JOB

POSITION: _____

RESPONSIBILITIES/DUTIES: _____
_____
_____
_____
_____
_____
_____

AGE: _____

LOCATION: _____

HIGHLIGHTS/ACCOMPLISHMENTS: _____
_____
_____
_____
_____
_____
_____

NOTES: _____
_____
_____
_____

FANTASY JOB

Imagine that you are given the opportunity, for one year, to hold any job or position you desire. You could be the president of the country, a research scientist, a ballet dancer, a sports writer, or a wilderness guide—anything you want. During this period you would not have to worry about finances or how the job would affect your personal or professional life.

What job or position would you choose?

What age would you be?

What would you hope to accomplish, learn, or do in that year?

	FRIDAY	SATURDAY	SUNDAY
6:00 A.M.			
7:00 A.M.			
8:00 A.M.			
9:00 A.M.			
10:00 A.M.			
11:00 A.M.			
12:00 P.M.			
1:00 P.M.			
2:00 P.M.			
3:00 P.M.			
4:00 P.M.			
5:00 P.M.			
6:00 P.M.			
7:00 P.M.			
8:00 P.M.			
9:00 P.M.			
10:00 P.M.			
11:00 P.M.			
12:00 A.M.			
1:00 A.M.			
2:00 A.M.			

IDEAL WEEKEND

What would make a weekend perfect for you at this time in your life? Describe, in detail, how you would ideally spend the hours from Friday evening through Sunday evening.

Would you be at home or away?

What activities would you choose?

How much time would you spend with family? Friends? Your partner?

How much time would you be by yourself?

IDEAL WEEKEND

	FRIDAY	SATURDAY	SUNDAY
6:00 A.M.			
7:00 A.M.			
8:00 A.M.			
9:00 A.M.			
10:00 A.M.			
11:00 A.M.			
12:00 P.M.			
1:00 P.M.			
2:00 P.M.			
3:00 P.M.			
4:00 P.M.			
5:00 P.M.			
6:00 P.M.			
7:00 P.M.			
8:00 P.M.			
9:00 P.M.			
10:00 P.M.			
11:00 P.M.			
12:00 A.M.			
1:00 A.M.			
2:00 A.M.			

IDEAL WEEKEND

What would make a weekend perfect for you at this time in your life? Describe, in detail, how you would ideally spend the hours from Friday evening through Sunday evening.

Would you be at home or away?

What activities would you choose?

How much time would you spend with family? Friends? Your partner?

How much time would you be by yourself?

RESEARCH AND DEVELOPMENT

	LEISURE ACTIVITIES	WHEN/HOW OFTEN	MINE	OURS
T H I S Y E A R				

F U T U R E				

RESEARCH AND DEVELOPMENT

Think about the cultural, recreational, athletic, philanthropic, educational, religious, or political activities that interest you.

What are the leisure-time interests or activities you would like to pursue in the coming year, alone or with your partner?

What leisure-time activities would you like to pursue at some time in your life, alone or with your partner?

RESEARCH AND DEVELOPMENT

	LEISURE ACTIVITIES	WHEN/HOW OFTEN	MINE	OURS
T H I S Y E A R				
F U T U R E				

RESEARCH AND DEVELOPMENT

Think about the cultural, recreational, athletic, philanthropic, educational, religious, or political activities that interest you.

What are the leisure-time interests or activities you would like to pursue in the coming year, alone or with your partner?

What leisure-time activities would you like to pursue at some time in your life, alone or with your partner?

ONE ENCHANTED EVENING

MY ENCHANTED EVENING WOULD BEGIN ABOUT ___ O'CLOCK

ONE ENCHANTED EVENING

Describe a romantic evening that fulfills your deepest desires or wildest fantasies.

When would it start?

What would you each be wearing?

Where would you go?

What would you do?

ONE ENCHANTED EVENING

MY ENCHANTED EVENING WOULD BEGIN ABOUT ___ O'CLOCK

ONE ENCHANTED EVENING

Describe a romantic evening that fulfills your deepest desires or wildest fantasies.

When would it start?

What would you each be wearing?

Where would you go?

What would you do?

	SEX	ROMANCE
FIVE THINGS I WOULD LIKE YOU TO DO MORE OFTEN	1. _____ 2. _____ 3. _____ 4. _____ 5. _____	_____ _____ _____ _____ _____
FIVE THINGS I THINK YOU WOULD LIKE ME TO DO MORE OFTEN	1. _____ 2. _____ 3. _____ 4. _____ 5. _____	_____ _____ _____ _____ _____
FIVE THINGS I WOULD LIKE TO DO ALONE WITH YOU MORE OFTEN	1. _____ 2. _____ 3. _____ 4. _____ 5. _____	

TRADE SECRETS

List five things you would like your partner to do more often related to sex and romance.

List five things you think your partner would like you to do more often related to sex and romance.

List five things you would like to do alone with your partner more often.

	SEX	ROMANCE
FIVE THINGS I WOULD LIKE YOU TO DO MORE OFTEN	1. _____ 2. _____ 3. _____ 4. _____ 5. _____	_____ _____ _____ _____ _____
FIVE THINGS I THINK YOU WOULD LIKE ME TO DO MORE OFTEN	1. _____ 2. _____ 3. _____ 4. _____ 5. _____	_____ _____ _____ _____ _____
FIVE THINGS I WOULD LIKE TO DO ALONE WITH YOU MORE OFTEN	1. _____ 2. _____ 3. _____ 4. _____ 5. _____	

TRADE SECRETS

List five things you would like your partner to do more often related to sex and romance.

List five things you think your partner would like you to do more often related to sex and romance.

List five things you would like to do alone with your partner more often.

SWEAT EQUITY

TASK	WHO DOES	RATING (1–5) TODAY	FUTURE	HOW TO ACHIEVE

PET PEEVES

HOME PROJECTS
THIS YEAR
WHAT   WHEN

FUTURE
WHAT   WHEN

SWEAT EQUITY

Develop a list of domestic responsibilities relevant to your household.

Indicate who is currently responsible for each chore. If shared, note what percentage each partner performs.

Using a scale of 1–5 (1 = low, 5 = high), rate how satisfied you are with the current state of affairs, what level you would like to reach in the coming year, and how you could achieve that.

List your pet peeves around the house.

List top-priority domestic projects for the coming year and for the future.

SWEAT EQUITY

TASK	WHO DOES	RATING (1–5) TODAY	FUTURE	HOW TO ACHIEVE

PET PEEVES

HOME PROJECTS
THIS YEAR
WHAT   WHEN

FUTURE
WHAT   WHEN

SWEAT EQUITY

Develop a list of domestic responsibilities relevant to your household.

Indicate who is currently responsible for each chore. If shared, note what percentage each partner performs.

Using a scale of 1–5 (1 = low, 5 = high), rate how satisfied you are with the current state of affairs, what level you would like to reach in the coming year, and how you could achieve that.

List your pet peeves around the house.

List top-priority domestic projects for the coming year and for the future.

CASH FLOW

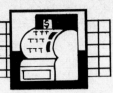

RATE YOUR SATISFACTION WITH:	1	2	3	4	5	WHAT WOULD YOU CHANGE?
INCOME						
THE WAY SPENDING DECISIONS ARE MADE						
SAVINGS AND INVESTMENTS						

PERCENTAGE OF JOINT INCOME SPENT ON:

RENT/MORTGAGE   _____

DINING OUT   _____

GROCERIES   _____

CLOTHING (ME)   _____

CLOTHING (YOU)   _____

CHILD CARE   _____

DOMESTIC HELP   _____

RECREATION   _____

TRAVEL/VACATIONS   _____

UTILITIES/PHONE   _____

TRANSPORTATION/CAR   _____

PERSONAL CARE (ME)   _____

PERSONAL CARE (YOU)   _____

MEDICAL/DENTAL   _____

PSYCHOLOGICAL

LOAN REPAYMENT/ INTEREST   _____

LEGAL/TAX/FINANCIAL   _____

_____

_____

_____

_____

_____

    = 100%

PET PEEVES ABOUT MONEY

_____
_____
_____
_____
_____
_____
_____
_____
_____
_____
_____
_____

MAJOR PURCHASES I WOULD LIKE TO MAKE

THIS YEAR   NEXT 5 YEARS

_____
_____
_____
_____
_____
_____
_____
_____
_____
_____

HOW DO YOU FEEL ABOUT YOUR CURRENT BUDGET?

CASH FLOW

Using a scale of 1–5 (1 = low, 5 = high), rate your satisfaction with your income situation, the way spending decisions are made in your partnership, and your savings and investment situation. What, if anything, would you change?

Fill out the spending chart to the best of your knowledge. How do you feel about this outflow of cash?

List your pet peeves about money in your partnership.

List major purchases you would like to make in the coming year and in the next five years.

CASH FLOW

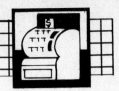

RATE YOUR SATISFACTION WITH:	1	2	3	4	5	WHAT WOULD YOU CHANGE?
INCOME						
THE WAY SPENDING DECISIONS ARE MADE						
SAVINGS AND INVESTMENTS						

PERCENTAGE OF JOINT INCOME SPENT ON:

RENT/MORTGAGE _____

DINING OUT _____

GROCERIES _____

CLOTHING (ME) _____

CLOTHING (YOU) _____

CHILD CARE _____

DOMESTIC HELP _____

RECREATION _____

TRAVEL/VACATIONS _____

UTILITIES/PHONE _____

TRANSPORTATION/CAR _____

PERSONAL CARE (ME) _____

PERSONAL CARE (YOU) _____

MEDICAL/DENTAL _____

PSYCHOLOGICAL _____

LOAN REPAYMENT/ INTEREST _____

LEGAL/TAX/FINANCIAL _____

_____ _____

_____ _____

_____ _____

_____ _____

_____ _____

= 100%

PET PEEVES ABOUT MONEY

_____
_____
_____
_____
_____
_____
_____
_____
_____
_____
_____
_____

MAJOR PURCHASES I WOULD LIKE TO MAKE

THIS YEAR   NEXT 5 YEARS

_____
_____
_____
_____
_____
_____
_____
_____
_____
_____
_____

HOW DO YOU FEEL ABOUT YOUR CURRENT BUDGET?

CASH FLOW

Using a scale of 1–5 (1 = low, 5 = high), rate your satisfaction with your income situation, the way spending decisions are made in your partnership, and your savings and investment situation. What, if anything, would you change?

Fill out the spending chart to the best of your knowledge. How do you feel about this outflow of cash?

List your pet peeves about money in your partnership.

List major purchases you would like to make in the coming year and in the next five years.

THE FAMILY BUSINESS

FAMILY MEMBER	ACTION	PERSON RESPONSIBLE

TIME TO BE SPENT WITH FAMILY MEMBERS THIS YEAR		
WHO	WHEN	WHERE

THE FAMILY BUSINESS

List the names of all family members with whom you would like to or feel obliged to stay in touch. (Exclude your partner and children living with you.)

Note what action you think should be taken with regard to each person and who you think should assume responsibility for fulfilling that action.

Describe when and where you would like to see important members of your families in the coming year.

FAMILY MEMBER	ACTION	PERSON RESPONSIBLE

TIME TO BE SPENT WITH FAMILY MEMBERS THIS YEAR		
WHO	WHEN	WHERE

THE FAMILY BUSINESS

List the names of all family members with whom you would like to or feel obliged to stay in touch. (Exclude your partner and children living with you.)

Note what action you think should be taken with regard to each person and who you think should assume responsibility for fulfilling that action.

Describe when and where you would like to see important members of your families in the coming year.

JOT DOWN ANY THOUGHTS YOU WANT TO DISCUSS RELATED TO THIS TOPIC

DO YOU WANT TO HAVE CHILDREN?   **NO**

YES

WHAT CHANGES DO YOU THINK WILL OCCUR IN YOUR LIFE?

HOW DO YOU FEEL ABOUT THAT?

	YOU	YOUR PARTNER

WHAT ROLES DO YOU EXPECT TO PLAY IN RAISING YOUR CHILDREN?

WHAT FACTORS WILL INFLUENCE YOUR DECISION ABOUT THE TIMING AND SPACING OF CHILDREN?

HOW MANY CHILDREN WOULD YOU LIKE TO HAVE? WHEN?

OTHER ISSUES

PRODUCT PLANNING

Answer the questions on the exercise. Use additional sheets of paper if necessary.

PRODUCT PLANNING

JOT DOWN ANY THOUGHTS YOU WANT TO DISCUSS
RELATED TO THIS TOPIC

DO YOU WANT TO HAVE
CHILDREN?   **NO**

YES

WHAT CHANGES DO
YOU THINK WILL OCCUR
IN YOUR LIFE?

HOW DO YOU
FEEL ABOUT THAT?

YOU   YOUR PARTNER

WHAT ROLES DO
YOU EXPECT TO
PLAY IN RAISING
YOUR CHILDREN?

WHAT FACTORS WILL
INFLUENCE YOUR
DECISION ABOUT THE
TIMING AND SPACING
OF CHILDREN?

HOW MANY CHILDREN
WOULD YOU LIKE TO HAVE?
WHEN?

OTHER ISSUES

PRODUCT PLANNING

Answer the questions on the exercise. Use additional sheets of paper if necessary.

PERSONNEL MANAGEMENT

TASK	PERSON RESPONSIBLE	SATIS-FACTION (1-5)	POSSIBLE SATIS-FACTION (1-5)	HOW

CONCERNS/
PROBLEM AREAS

GOALS—THIS YEAR

GOALS—FUTURE

PET PEEVES

CONCERNS ABOUT PARENTING AND MY PARTNERSHIP

PERSONNEL MANAGEMENT

Develop a list of parenting tasks and responsibilities relevant to your life.

For each duty, note who is responsible. If shared, indicate the percentage each partner performs.

Using a scale of 1–5 (1 = low, 5 = high), rate your level of satisfaction with the current situation, note what you would like to achieve in the coming year and how it could be accomplished.

How do parenting responsibilities affect your relationship with your partner? Jot down your thoughts.

List any concerns you may have about your child(ren) and any problem areas that need attention.

List any goals you have for your child(ren) for the coming year and the future.

List your pet peeves about parenting and/or your child(ren).

PERSONNEL MANAGEMENT

TASK	PERSON RESPONSIBLE	SATIS-FACTION (1-5)	POSSIBLE SATIS-FACTION (1-5)	HOW

CONCERNS/ PROBLEM AREAS

GOALS—THIS YEAR

GOALS—FUTURE

PET PEEVES

CONCERNS ABOUT PARENTING AND MY PARTNERSHIP

PERSONNEL MANAGEMENT

Develop a list of parenting tasks and responsibilities relevant to your life.

For each duty, note who is responsible. If shared, indicate the percentage each partner performs.

Using a scale of 1–5 (1 = low, 5 = high), rate your level of satisfaction with the current situation, note what you would like to achieve in the coming year and how it could be accomplished.

How do parenting responsibilities affect your relationship with your partner? Jot down your thoughts.

List any concerns you may have about your child(ren) and any problem areas that need attention.

List any goals you have for your child(ren) for the coming year and the future.

List your pet peeves about parenting and/or your child(ren).

PHYSICAL INVENTORY

	A⁺	A	A⁻	B⁺	B	B⁻	C⁺	C	C⁻	D	F	GRADE NEXT YEAR	STRATEGY FOR MAKING THE GRADE
EATING HABITS/NUTRITION													
EXERCISE													
WEIGHT													
SLEEP													
DENTAL													
MEDICAL													
ALCOHOL													
STRESS													
DRUGS													
EYES													
GROOMING/ IMAGE													

LONG-TERM HEALTH GOALS	TIME FRAME

PHYSICAL INVENTORY

Think of all the things that make up your sense of health and well-being. Add any other categories to the list.

Grade yourself in each category.

Indicate the grade you would like to make next year.

What will you have to do to make that grade?

List long-term health goals and related time frames.

PHYSICAL INVENTORY

	A⁺	A	A⁻	B⁺	B	B⁻	C⁺	C	C⁻	D	F	GRADE NEXT YEAR	STRATEGY FOR MAKING THE GRADE
EATING HABITS/NUTRITION													
EXERCISE													
WEIGHT													
SLEEP													
DENTAL													
MEDICAL													
ALCOHOL													
STRESS													
DRUGS													
EYES													
GROOMING/ IMAGE													

LONG-TERM HEALTH GOALS	TIME FRAME
_____	_____
_____	_____
_____	_____

PHYSICAL INVENTORY

Think of all the things that make up your sense of health and well-being. Add any other categories to the list.

Grade yourself in each category.

Indicate the grade you would like to make next year.

What will you have to do to make that grade?

List long-term health goals and related time frames.

LEAVE OF ABSENCE

TRIPS — EXCURSIONS — ADVENTURES

THIS YEAR		FUTURE	
WHERE	WHEN	WHERE	WHEN

MY IDEAL VACATION

LEAVE OF ABSENCE

List all the trips, excursions, and adventures you would like to take this year. Indicate a preferred time.

List all the trips, excursions, and adventures you would like to make some time in your life.

Describe your ideal vacation.

    How long would it be?

    Where would you go?

    With whom would you be?

LEAVE OF ABSENCE

TRIPS — EXCURSIONS — ADVENTURES

THIS YEAR		FUTURE	
WHERE	WHEN	WHERE	WHEN

MY IDEAL VACATION

LEAVE OF ABSENCE

List all the trips, excursions, and adventures you would like to take this year. Indicate a preferred time.

List all the trips, excursions, and adventures you would like to make some time in your life.

Describe your ideal vacation.

How long would it be?

Where would you go?

With whom would you be?

ENVIRONMENTAL EFFECTS

TIME OF LIFE	TYPE OF DWELLING	NEIGHBORHOOD	COMMUNITY	GEOGRAPHIC AREA

PLACES I WOULD LIKE TO LIVE SOMETIME

WHERE	WHEN

ENVIRONMENTAL EFFECTS

Think about the environmental characteristics that would be most conducive to your happiness and well-being at various times in your life. List them for each of the following categories.

Dwelling   Size, kind of space, maintenance
Neighborhood   Ethnic mix, age group, type of homes
Community   Schools, political climate, services
Geographic area Climate, recreational opportunities, life-style

Are there cities, states, or parts of the world where you would like to live for a period of time? Note where and when.

ENVIRONMENTAL EFFECTS

TIME OF LIFE	TYPE OF DWELLING	NEIGHBORHOOD	COMMUNITY	GEOGRAPHIC AREA

PLACES I WOULD LIKE TO LIVE SOMETIME

WHERE	WHEN

ENVIRONMENTAL EFFECTS

Think about the environmental characteristics that would be most conducive to your happiness and well-being at various times in your life. List them for each of the following categories.

Dwelling   Size, kind of space, maintenance
Neighborhood   Ethnic mix, age group, type of homes
Community   Schools, political climate, services
Geographic area Climate, recreational opportunities, life-style

Are there cities, states, or parts of the world where you would like to live for a period of time? Note where and when.

THE COMPANY WE KEEP

BEST FRIENDS

MINE	OURS

GOOD FRIENDS

MINE	OURS

CASUAL FRIENDS

MINE	OURS

BUSINESS AND PROFESSIONAL FRIENDS

MINE	OURS

PEOPLE TO GET TO KNOW BETTER

ME	US

THE COMPANY WE KEEP

According to the definitions below (which you should feel free to modify in any way) list your friends and acquaintances in the most appropriate box. Distinguish between your personal friends and friends you share as a couple.

BEST FRIENDS: These people are extra special. Even if you do not see each other often, the relationship always feels easy, comfortable, and intimate. You would do anything for these friends and know they would do the same for you.

GOOD FRIENDS: Friends with whom you have a strong and healthy relationship that you desire to maintain. To that end, you are willing to invest a fair amount of time and energy in getting together and staying in touch.

CASUAL FRIENDS: People who are lower on your priority list. Perhaps you see them socially on occasion, but you are not interested in going out of your way to get together.

BUSINESS AND PROFESSIONAL FRIENDS: People with whom you want to spend time for business or professional reasons.

PEOPLE TO GET TO KNOW: These are folks you would like to get to know better. You are willing to make a special effort to explore and develop what you believe might be an interesting friendship.

BEST FRIENDS

MINE	OURS

GOOD FRIENDS

MINE	OURS

CASUAL FRIENDS

MINE	OURS

BUSINESS AND PROFESSIONAL FRIENDS

MINE	OURS

PEOPLE TO GET TO KNOW BETTER

ME	US

THE COMPANY WE KEEP

According to the definitions below (which you should feel free to modify in any way) list your friends and acquaintances in the most appropriate box. Distinguish between your personal friends and friends you share as a couple.

BEST FRIENDS: These people are extra special. Even if you do not see each other often, the relationship always feels easy, comfortable, and intimate. You would do anything for these friends and know they would do the same for you.

GOOD FRIENDS: Friends with whom you have a strong and healthy relationship that you desire to maintain. To that end, you are willing to invest a fair amount of time and energy in getting together and staying in touch.

CASUAL FRIENDS: People who are lower on your priority list. Perhaps you see them socially on occasion, but you are not interested in going out of your way to get together.

BUSINESS AND PROFESSIONAL FRIENDS: People with whom you want to spend time for business or professional reasons.

PEOPLE TO GET TO KNOW: These are folks you would like to get to know better. You are willing to make a special effort to explore and develop what you believe might be an interesting friendship.

THE SUMMIT MEETING

SUMMIT TIMETABLE

DAY	TIME	ACTIVITY	DETAILS

SUMMIT TIMETABLE

Using the Summit Talk Agenda and Summit Logistics Planner you completed at your Planning Meeting, fill out the Summit Timetable; account for all the time from now until you depart. Include specific details for Summit Talk, recreation, special activities, and meals.

We recommend that you initially allow the following times for your Summit Talk:

Getting Started   1–2 hours

Discussion and Decision-Making   8–10 hours (approximately one hour for
                                                                         each functional area)

Wrap-Up   1–2 hours

You can modify and revise your timetable at any time during your Summit.

SUMMIT GROUND RULES

Take a few minutes to share your thoughts about the hours ahead. How are you feeling?

Based upon these feelings, your knowledge of yourselves, and past experiences in communicating, are there ground rules you feel would facilitate your discussions?

Think about words, phrases, references, gestures, behaviors, or tone of voice that hit a "hot button" for either of you. You may want to develop ground rules that ban those from your Summit.

Think about words, references, gestures, and behaviors that are particularly positive or reassuring for you. You may want to develop ground rules that encourage those at your Summit.

List your ground rules.

THINGS I LIKE

THINGS I LIKE ABOUT

1.

2.

3.

4.

5.

6.

7.

8.

9.

10.

THINGS I LIKE ABOUT

1.

2.

3.

4.

5.

6.

7.

8.

9.

10.

THINGS I LIKE

List ten things you love about your partner on a separate sheet of paper.

Read your lists to each other.

Copy your list onto the exercise sheet and refer to it if necessary at your Summit.

ACTION PLAN: OVERVIEW

NOTES:

DISCUSSION GUIDELINES: OVERVIEW

The three exercises included in this Discussion Guideline are designed to give you the "big picture" of your life: the way you would like to remember it when you look back, the way you would like to see it unfold, and the way you feel about it now. Each of these exercises will generate a lot of discussion. If possible, save detailed discussion about these exercises until later, when you will talk in depth about specific issues they raise. For now, simply share and talk briefly about each exercise in turn.

HAPPINESS SCALE
- Share your exercises.
- Talk briefly about the rating scale you used to measure your level of happiness.

PERSONAL TIMELINE
- Share your exercises.
- Superimpose one Personal Timeline on the other. Are they compatible? What are the major differences and similarities?

OBITUARY
- Share your exercises.
- Are you surprised at what you included or excluded from your obituary?
- Are you surprised at what your partner included or excluded?

Keep these three exercises handy as you talk about all of the functional areas. You will want to refer to them throughout your Summit Talk.

ACTION PLAN: WORK

THINGS I COULD DO TO GET CLOSER TO MY IDEAL WEEK:

NAME: _____   NAME: _____

_____   _____
_____   _____
_____   _____
_____   _____
_____   _____
_____   _____
_____   _____
_____   _____
_____   _____
_____   _____
_____   _____
_____   _____
_____   _____
_____   _____
_____   _____
_____   _____
_____   _____
_____   _____

NOTES: _____

_____
_____
_____
_____
_____
_____
_____
_____

DISCUSSION GUIDELINES: WORK

HAPPINESS SCALE
- Why did you rate your level of satisfaction as you did?

IDEAL WORKWEEK
- What are the differences and similarities between your ideal workweek and a typical week now?

- How does your ideal week differ from your partner's? How is it similar?

- What does your description suggest about your interests and work style?

- What aspects of your current workweek (commute, location, people, duties) do you most enjoy? Least enjoy?

- Are there things you could do to make your current workweek more like your ideal? List those on the Action Plan.

FANTASY JOB

- Share and discuss your exercises.

- Are there surprises for either of you?

- What does your fantasy job say about your desires?

- Is there any chance your fantasy job might become a reality? How could you make it happen?

PERSONAL TIMELINE

- Talk about the career path you have outlined.

- How do your career aspirations mesh with your partner's?

- What factors most influence decisions (relocation, job change, time off) you make about your career?

- Do you anticipate a job or career change in the near or long-term future? If so, when? What will it be?

PERSONAL AGENDA ITEMS
Review your Summit Talk Agenda. Discuss any agenda items related to this functional area. List resolutions, actions, and plans on your Action Plan.

ACTION PLAN: LEISURE

THINGS WE COULD DO TO MAKE THE WEEKEND MORE IDEAL:

_____
_____
_____
_____
_____
_____
_____
_____
_____
_____
_____

ACTIVITIES/INTERESTS WE WILL PURSUE THIS YEAR:

NAME	ACTIVITY	HOW OFTEN/WHEN

ACTIVITIES/INTERESTS WE WILL PURSUE TOGETHER THIS YEAR:

ACTIVITY	HOW OFTEN/WHEN

NOTES: _____
_____
_____
_____

DISCUSSION GUIDELINES: LEISURE

HAPPINESS SCALE
- Why did you rate your level of satisfaction as you did?

IDEAL WEEKEND
- How is your ideal weekend different from a typical weekend now?
- How does your ideal weekend differ from your partner's? What does that say about your interests, values, and priorities?
- List on your Action Plan things you could do to make your weekends more ideal.

RESEARCH AND DEVELOPMENT
- Share and discuss your exercises.
- How do your interests compare with your partner's? Are there any shared interests?
- What, if any, changes must you make in order to pursue the interests and activities you desire?
- On your Action Plan, list the activities and interests you *will* pursue this year, alone and together.
- What are the major activities you would like to pursue in your lifetime? When? What will it take to do so?

PERSONAL AGENDA ITEMS
Review your Summit Talk Agenda. Discuss any agenda items related to this functional area. List resolutions, actions, and plans on your Action Plan.

ACTION PLAN: LOVE

ENCHANTED EVENING

PLANNED BY: _____

MONTH: _____

ONE THING I (_____)

WILL TRY TO DO MORE OFTEN:

SEX: _____
_____

ROMANCE: _____
_____

ENCHANTED EVENING

PLANNED BY _____

MONTH: _____

ONE THING I (_____)

WILL TRY TO DO MORE OFTEN:

SEX: _____
_____

ROMANCE: _____
_____

TWO THINGS WE WILL DO TOGETHER MORE OFTEN

WHAT: _____
_____
_____
_____

WHEN/HOW OFTEN: _____
_____
_____
_____

WHAT: _____
_____
_____
_____

WHEN/HOW OFTEN: _____
_____
_____
_____

NOTES: _____
_____
_____
_____
_____
_____
_____
_____
_____
_____

DISCUSSION GUIDELINES: LOVE

HAPPINESS SCALE
- Why did you rate yourself at that level of satisfaction?

ONE ENCHANTED EVENING
- Share your exercises. What does your romantic evening say about you?
- How is your romantic evening different from or similar to your partner's?
- Pick a date when you will make your partner's enchanted evening (or something close to it) a reality. Note on your Action Plan.

TRADE SECRETS
- How do your desires differ?
- How do you feel about the desires your partner expressed? Can you do those things more often?
- Choose something you will try to do more often in the areas of sex and romance. Add to your Action Plan.
- How do the things you said you would like to do more often compare with your partner's ideas?
- Choose two things you will try to do more often together in the coming year. Note on your Action Plan.

PERSONAL AGENDA ITEMS
Review your Summit Talk Agenda. Discuss any agenda items related to this functional area. List resolutions, actions, and plans on your Action Plan.

TASK	PERSON RESPONSIBLE	GUIDELINES (HOW OFTEN, WHEN, STANDARDS)

PRIORITY HOME PROJECTS

PROJECT	TIME FRAME	PERSON RESPONSIBLE

NOTES: _____

DISCUSSION GUIDELINES: HOME

HAPPINESS SCALE
- Why did you rate yourself at that level of satisfaction?

SWEAT EQUITY
- Share your responses.
- Approximately what percentage of the responsibility for home care do each of you assume?
- How do you feel about that arrangement? Why?
- Are there areas that cause particular problems? Which ones?
- Are there feasible solutions to those problems? What are they? What compromises or trade-offs must be made? By whom?
- What can you say about your expectations for home care? Do they differ from your partner's?
- Talk about your pet peeves and ways to address them.
- Discuss and agree on who does what. On your Action Plan list tasks, the person responsible, and guidelines for completion.
- On your Action Plan list any priority home projects you agree to complete.

PERSONAL AGENDA ITEMS
Review your Summit Talk Agenda. Discuss any agenda items related to this functional area. List resolutions, actions, and plans on your Action Plan.

ACTION PLAN: MONEY

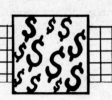

BUDGET RESOLUTIONS: _____
_____
_____
_____
_____
_____
_____

SPENDING DECISIONS RESOLUTIONS: ____
_____
_____
_____
_____
_____
_____

INCOME RESOLUTIONS: _____
_____
_____
_____
_____
_____
_____
_____

SAVINGS/INVESTMENT RESOLUTIONS: ____
_____
_____
_____
_____
_____
_____
_____

MAJOR PURCHASES/EXPENDITURES

THIS YEAR:

WHAT	COST	WHEN

NEXT 5 YEARS:

WHAT	COST	WHEN

NOTES: _____
_____
_____
_____

DISCUSSION GUIDELINES: MONEY

HAPPINESS SCALE
- Why did you rate yourself at that level of satisfaction?

CASH FLOW
- Share your exercises.
- How do you feel about your budget? What would you change? Note resolutions on your Action Plan.
- How do you feel about the way spending decisions are made? What would you change? Note resolutions on your Action Plan.
- How do you feel about the income to your partnership? What would you change? Is that possible? How?
- How do you feel about your savings and investment situation? What would you change? Note resolutions on your Action Plan.
- Share your pet peeves about money or finances.
- Share your consumer desires. List the major purchases you hope to make in the coming year and next five years.

PERSONAL TIMELINE
- What do you hope or plan to receive in total income at various points on your timeline?

PERSONAL AGENDA ITEMS
Review your Summit Talk Agenda. Discuss any agenda items related to this functional area. List resolutions, actions, and plans on your Action Plan.

ACTION PLAN: FAMILY

FAMILY: THE FAMILY BUSINESS

FAMILY MEMBER	ACTION	PERSON RESPONSIBLE

TIME WITH FAMILY THIS YEAR

WHO	WHEN	WHERE

NOTES: _____
_____
_____
_____
_____

DISCUSSION GUIDELINES: FAMILY

HAPPINESS SCALE
- Why did you rate yourself at that level of satisfaction?

THE FAMILY BUSINESS
- Fill in the names of all family members from your individual exercises on the Action Plan.
- Decide what action will fulfill your commitment or obligation to each family member. Note on your Action Plan.
- Decide who will be responsible for that action. Note on your Action Plan.
- Set tentative dates for visits with important family members.

PRODUCT PLANNING
- Discuss your responses to the exercise.
- How do your responses differ?
- Will you have children? How many? When?

PERSONNEL MANAGEMENT
- What percentage of the responsibility for child care do each of you assume?
- What is your overall level of satisfaction with this arrangement? Can you say why? What areas are particularly unsatisfactory?
- Realistically, what could your overall level of satisfaction be? How?
- Negotiate any changes that must be made. Note specific responsibilities on the Action Plan.
- Note resolutions related to parenting on the Action Plan.
- For each child, discuss goals and ways to achieve them. List strategies on Action Plan.
- Discuss your pet peeves and ways to address them.

PERSONAL AGENDA ITEMS
Review your Summit Talk Agenda. Discuss any agenda items related to this functional area. List resolutions, actions, and plans on your Action Plan.

FAMILY: PRODUCT PLANNING

NOTES:

FAMILY: PERSONNEL MANAGEMENT

TASK	PERSON RESPONSIBLE	GUIDELINES

PARENTING RESOLUTIONS: _____

_____

_____

_____

_____

_____

CHILD GOALS

_____

_____

_____

_____

STRATEGY

_____

_____

_____

_____

NOTES: _____

_____

_____

_____

ACTION PLAN: HEALTH

NAME: _____
ACTION

WHEN/HOW OFTEN

NAME: _____
ACTION

WHEN/HOW OFTEN

NOTES: _____

DISCUSSION GUIDELINES: HEALTH

HAPPINESS SCALE
- Why did you rate yourself at that level of satisfaction?

PHYSICAL INVENTORY
- Why did you give yourself those grades?
- Are any of the health components of greater or lesser importance to you? Why?
- On your Action Plan, list specific actions you will take in the coming year to help you make the grade.
- Talk about how your partner can help.

PERSONAL AGENDA ITEMS
Review your Summit Talk Agenda. Discuss any agenda items related to this functional area. List resolutions, actions, and plans on your Action Plan.

ACTION PLAN: TRAVEL

TRIPS/EXCURSIONS/ADVENTURES THIS YEAR:

WHAT/WHERE	WHEN	PLANNING TASKS

TRIPS/EXCURSIONS/ADVENTURES IN THE FUTURE:

WHAT/WHERE	WHEN

NOTES: _____

_____

_____

_____

_____

DISCUSSION GUIDELINES: TRAVEL

HAPPINESS SCALE
- Why did you rate yourself at that level of satisfaction?

LEAVE OF ABSENCE
- Share your ideal vacations. How are they alike? Different? What does your ideal vacation say about you?
- How do the places you would like to visit compare with your partner's choices?
- On your Action Plan, list the trips or excursions you will take this year. Who is responsible for planning them?
- What trips or vacations would you like to take in the future? When?

PERSONAL TIMELINE
- Do your travel plans and goals fit with other career and life-style considerations?

PERSONAL AGENDA ITEMS

Review your Summit Talk Agenda. Discuss any agenda items related to this functional area. List resolutions, actions, and plans on your Action Plan.

ACTION PLAN: ENVIRONMENT

THINGS WE COULD DO TO GET CLOSER TO OUR IDEAL ENVIRONMENT

WHAT

WHEN

_____   _____
_____   _____
_____   _____
_____   _____
_____   _____
_____   _____
_____   _____
_____   _____
_____   _____
_____   _____
_____   _____
_____   _____
_____   _____
_____   _____
_____   _____

PLACES WE WOULD LIKE TO LIVE SOMETIME

PLACE   TIME FRAME   STEPS TO GET THERE

_____   _____   _____
_____   _____   _____
_____   _____   _____
_____   _____   _____

NOTES: _____
_____
_____
_____
_____
_____
_____
_____

DISCUSSION GUIDELINES: ENVIRONMENT

HAPPINESS SCALE
- Why did you rate yourself at that level of satisfaction?

ENVIRONMENTAL EFFECTS
- Why are the characteristics you listed important to you?
- What are the differences and similarities between your preferences and those of your partner?
- How do the geographic area, community, neighborhood, and dwelling in which you are currently living compare with your ideal?
- On your Action Plan, list what you can do to get closer to your ideal.
- Are there places you both agree you would like to live sometime in your life?

PERSONAL TIMELINE
- At what points in your life do you hope to make major changes in your living situation?
- How do your geographic preferences mesh with your career and other life-style considerations? What trade-offs might you have to make to live exactly where you want?

PERSONAL AGENDA ITEMS
Review your Summit Talk Agenda. Discuss any agenda items related to this functional area. List resolutions, actions, and plans on your Action Plan.

_____'S PERSONAL FRIENDS

NAME	ACTION

_____'S PERSONAL FRIENDS

NAME	ACTION

BEST FRIENDS

NAME	ACTION

GOOD FRIENDS

NAME	ACTION

CASUAL FRIENDS

NAME	ACTION

BUSINESS AND PROFESSIONAL FRIENDS

NAME	ACTION

PEOPLE TO GET TO KNOW BETTER

NAME	ACTION

DISCUSSION GUIDELINES: FRIENDS

HAPPINESS SCALE
- Why did you rate yourself at that level of satisfaction?

THE COMPANY WE KEEP
- Share your exercises.
- Complete the Action Plan by agreeing upon what friends to put in each category.
- What actions will you take with your friends?

PERSONAL AGENDA ITEMS

Review your Summit Talk Agenda. Discuss any agenda items related to this functional area. List resolutions, actions, and plans on your Action Plan.

PRIORITY ACTION PLAN

NAME

_____

ACTION	TARGET DATE/ TIME FRAME

NAME

_____

ACTION	TARGET DATE/ TIME FRAME

PRIORITY ACTION PLAN

Review your Action Plans for each functional area and any other notes you made during your Summit Talk. Transfer important or top-priority resolutions and commitments to the Priority Action Plan. Make sure a target date or time frame accompanies each action and indicate who is responsible for making it happen.

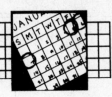
MONTH: _____

MONTH: _____

MONTH: _____

MONTH: _____

MONTH: _____

MONTH: _____

MONTH: _____

MONTH: _____

MONTH: _____

MONTH: _____

MONTH: _____

MONTH: _____

PLANNING CALENDAR

Using the notes and Action Plans from your Summit Talk, fill in each month of the Planning Calendar with highlights for the coming year. These may be confirmed events (e.g., a family wedding) or tentative plans that you would like to bring to fruition (e.g., winter helicopter skiing in Canada).

YEAR OR AGE	WORK	LEISURE	LOVE	HOME	MONEY	FAMILY	HEALTH	TRAVEL	ENVIRON-MENT	FRIENDS

MASTER TIMELINE

Taking into account all that you have discussed, map out your future together, as you see it at this moment, in as much or as little detail as you wish on the Master Timeline. Note major anticipated events for each functional area, such as the birth of children, career or job changes, major purchases, geographic moves, or anything that you feel represents a milestone in your life together.

KEY WORDS TO DESCRIBE OUR LIFE IN THE COMING YEAR:

KEY VALUES THAT WILL GUIDE OUR LIVES:

WORDS THAT DESCRIBE OUR SUMMIT:

THE MOST IMPORTANT THINGS WE LEARNED ABOUT OURSELVES:
NAME: NAME:

THE MOST IMPORTANT THINGS WE LEARNED ABOUT EACH OTHER:
NAME: NAME:

THE MOST IMPORTANT THINGS WE LEARNED ABOUT OUR RELATIONSHIP:

DATE FOR FOLLOW-UP MEETING:

SUMMING IT UP

Together, answer the questions on the exercise.

MANAGING YOUR LIFE TOGETHER

FOLLOW-UP EXERCISE

NOW THAT YOU HAVE HAD SOME TIME TO REFLECT ON YOUR SUMMIT MEETING, HOW DO YOU FEEL ABOUT THE EXPERIENCE?

WOULD YOU LIKE TO DO IT AGAIN?

WHAT WOULD YOU CHANGE NEXT TIME?

HOW DO YOU FEEL ABOUT YOUR PROGRESS SINCE YOU RETURNED HOME?

WHAT ARE THE GREATEST SUCCESSES?

WHAT ARE THE GREATEST DISAPPOINTMENTS?

CAN YOU RESOLVE ANY OF THE DISAPPOINTMENTS? HOW?

ARE THERE ANY ITEMS ON YOUR PRIORITY ACTION PLAN OR PLANNING CALENDAR THAT NEED REVISION AT THIS POINT? WHAT ARE THEY?

OTHER DISCUSSION ITEMS:

FOLLOW-UP EXERCISE

Answer the questions on the exercise.

List any other specific issues you would like to discuss at the Follow-Up Meeting.

NOW THAT YOU HAVE HAD SOME TIME TO REFLECT ON YOUR SUMMIT MEETING, HOW DO YOU FEEL ABOUT THE EXPERIENCE?

WOULD YOU LIKE TO DO IT AGAIN?

WHAT WOULD YOU CHANGE NEXT TIME?

HOW DO YOU FEEL ABOUT YOUR PROGRESS SINCE YOU RETURNED HOME?

WHAT ARE THE GREATEST SUCCESSES?

WHAT ARE THE GREATEST DISAPPOINTMENTS?

CAN YOU RESOLVE ANY OF THE DISAPPOINTMENTS? HOW?

ARE THERE ANY ITEMS ON YOUR PRIORITY ACTION PLAN OR PLANNING CALENDAR THAT NEED REVISION AT THIS POINT? WHAT ARE THEY?

OTHER DISCUSSION ITEMS:

FOLLOW-UP EXERCISE

Answer the questions on the exercise.

List any other specific issues ycu would like to discuss at the Follow-Up Meeting.

FOLLOW-UP ACTION PLAN

DATE FOR OUR NEXT SUMMIT MEETING _____

DATE FOR AN INTERIM MINI-SUMMIT _____

TIME AND PLACE FOR A PARTNERS' MEETING _____

NOTES: _____
_____
_____
_____
_____
_____
_____
_____
_____
_____
_____
_____
_____
_____
_____
_____
_____
_____
_____
_____
_____
_____

DISCUSSION GUIDELINES: FOLLOW-UP MEETING

Share and discuss your responses to the Follow-Up Exercise.

Talk about any other issues of interest or concern.

If you decide to have an annual Summit, pick a tentative date.

If you decide to have an interim Mini-Summit, select a tentative date.

If you decide to have a regular partners' meeting, agree upon a time to hold it.

We hope your first Summit was a success and that you learned some things about yourselves and your relationship that will enrich your partnership. You are on your own now: continue to integrate the Summit process into your lives and build together a healthy, happy *working* relationship.